I BELIEVE

EXPERIENCE HIM. SHARE HIM.

GOD'S WORD on TRUTH,
JESUS, Love, Fear,
School, FRIENDS, CHURCH,
and Living Life

TERRY BROWN
AND MICHAEL ROSS

BARBOUR
PUBLISHING

Published by Barbour Publishing, Inc., P.O. Box 719, Uhrichsville, Ohio 44683, www.barbourbooks.com

Member of the
Evangelical Christian
Publishers Association

Printed in the United States of America.

5 4 3 2 1

Dedicated to the memory
of Nicki Carol Turner
who touched and healed many lives. . .
a friend who believed in God's promises.

—Terry Brown

To Floyd Cox. You are my role model—
a man with a heart for evangelism and
a reverence for God's holy Word.

—Michael Ross

contents

how to use this book

You're about to begin a life-changing journey through Scripture.

God's Word is powerful—"sharper than any double-edged sword" (Hebrews 4:12 NIV). When Jesus was battling it out with Satan in the wilderness, it was the only weapon He chose to fight with. What makes the Holy Bible so amazing is that it's "God-breathed." Think about that for a minute. The all-powerful Creator of the universe breathed His very life into the words of Scripture. Something with that ultimate authority has to be life-changing!

the Bible says that God's Word:

- Cleans us up (Ephesians 5:26).
- Shows us what we're really like (James 1:23–25).
- Encourages us (Romans 15:4).
- Equips us to do good (2 Timothy 3:17).
- Leads us to faith (Romans 10:17).
- Shows us the way to be saved (James 1:21).

But face it: You need a Bible reference guide that's relevant, easy-to-read, and that you'll feel comfortable passing along to your friends—a book that's packed with the Word of God as well as insights from real people, not to mention practical tips and ideas on how you can apply Scripture to your life. Guess what? That's exactly what this resource is all about!

If *Communicate* is the book you read to learn how to live and share your faith, then *I Believe* is a handy "road map" that will guide you through key Bible truths. It's a book you can feel confident giving to your friends—especially those needing to learn more about Scripture, God, and relationships.

The Bible is relevant. It's the message we must communicate to the world. It speaks to the day-to-day issues that you face. *I Believe* shares the message that "you are not alone in the issues you encounter."

inside, you'll find. . .

- ❯ Topics from A to Z, arranged to confirm first what I Believe—God, Jesus, the Bible, and much more.

- ❯ Contemporary Bible references, including Scripture from THE MESSAGE.

- "Wisdom Past and Present": relevant insights from heroes of the faith.
- "Reality Bytes": real-life stories and testimonies from teens.
- "Truth Tips": practical ideas on how to apply God's Word to your life.

topics include:

- Who GOD Is—the nature of God, Jesus, the Holy Spirit, His will.
- What Is REAL—authenticity, truth, prayer, beliefs, heaven, hell, creation.
- I FEEL Like—emotions, feelings, thoughts, self-image.
- When It's HARD—school, parents, the future, pressure, fears.
- Why THEY Matter—community, church, friends, family, relationships.

chapter one

who God is

*Knowing God and
His Will for Your Life*

assurance

"My purpose is that they may
be encouraged in heart and united in love,
so that they may have the full riches of
complete understanding, in order that they
may know the mystery of God, namely,
Christ, in whom are hidden all the treasures
of wisdom and knowledge."

—Colossians 2:2–3 NIV

"Yet he. . .gave glory to God, being
fully persuaded that God had power to do
what he had promised."

—Romans 4:20–21 NIV

wisdom past and present

"The source of assurance, however, is not our
inferences as such, but the work of the Spirit, apart
from as well as through our inferences, convincing
us that we are God's children and that the saving
love and promises of God apply directly to us."

J. I. Packer, *Knowing God*

Ten Assurances About Christ

- He can be trusted.
- He is all-powerful.
- He is infinite.
- He is in control.
- He is the Source of truth.
- He accepts you.
- He loves you.
- He forgives you.
- He has an amazing plan for your life.
- He invites you to spend eternity with Him.

comfort

"Blessed be the God and Father of our
Lord Jesus Christ, the Father of mercies
and God of all comfort, who comforts
us in all our tribulation, that we may be able
to comfort those who are in any trouble,
with the comfort with which we ourselves
are comforted by God."

—2 Corinthians 1:3–4 NKJV

" 'You're blessed when you feel you've lost
what is most dear to you. Only then can you
be embraced by the One most dear to you.' "

—Matthew 5:4 THE MESSAGE

wisdom past and present

"Every time we let loneliness take over our feelings, we have lost sight of that personal, caring,
and loving Father. He is 'Abba,' our Papa. Even if
no other person understands or cares, He does.
That is the God Jesus fled to when He felt lonely.
The same caring Father is there for us."

Michael Card, *Immanuel: Reflections
on the Life of Christ*

truth tips

God Is Personal—The God Who Comforts

- God loves us, and He reaches out to us on a very personal level (Matthew 7:21).

- God is interactive (Matthew 6:10).

- God speaks and listens (Genesis 1:3, Psalm 94:9).

- God feels (Genesis 6:6, Deuteronomy 1:37, Exodus 20:5, Psalm 111:4).

- God has a name—He isn't just an "it" (Genesis 4:26, Exodus 20:7, Exodus 20:24, Exodus 23:21, Ezekiel 43:7-8).

- God created us (Acts 17:24, Ephesians 1:11).

who God is

compassion

"As you know, we consider blessed those
who have persevered. You have heard of
Job's perseverance and have seen what the
Lord finally brought about. The Lord is
full of compassion and mercy."

—James 5:11 NIV

"The Lord is good to all;
he has compassion on all he has made."

—Psalm 145:9 NIV

"Through the LORD's mercies
we are not consumed, because
His compassions fail not."

—Lamentations 3:22 NKJV

wisdom past and present

"We all long for heaven where God is, but we
have it in our power to be in heaven with Him
right now—to be happy with Him at this very
moment. But being happy with Him now means
loving like He loves, helping like He helps, giving

as He gives, serving as He serves, rescuing as He rescues, being with Him twenty-four hours a day—touching Him in His distressing disguise."

Mother Teresa, *Mother Teresa:
Contemplative in the Heart of the World*

truth tips

A Christian's Five-Point Call to Compassion

▶ Called to love (Romans 13:8)

▶ Called to set a good example (Romans 15:2)

▶ Called to serve (1 Peter 4:10)

▶ Called to support those in ministry
  (3 John 5–8)

▶ Called to help those in need
  (Acts 2:44–45)

who God is

creator

"In the beginning God created
the heavens and the earth."

—Genesis 1:1 NIV

"For by Him were all things created, that
are in heaven, and that are in earth, visible
and invisible, whether they be thrones, or
dominions, or principalities, or powers: all
things were created by him, and for him."

—Colossians 1:16 KJV

"Rain down, you heavens, from above,
and let the skies pour down righteousness;
let the earth open, let them bring forth
salvation, and let righteousness spring up
together. I, the LORD, have created it."

—Isaiah 45:8 NKJV

wisdom past and present

"All things, and specially Life, arose within Him, and
within Him all things will reach their conclusion—

the final statement of what they have been trying
to express."

C. S. Lewis, *Miracles*

truth tips

*Mind-Boggling Thoughts
about Our AWESOME Creator*

- He is the one and only God (Deuteronomy
  6:4, Isaiah 44:8).

- He is bigger than we could ever imagine
  (Psalm 145:3).

- He existed before the world, He exists now,
  and He will exist forever (Revelation 15:4,
  Jude 25, Psalm 102:27, Isaiah 40:28, Revelation
  1:4, Psalm 90:2).

- He is alive and all life flows from Him
  (Psalm 84:2, Isaiah 40:28, Psalm 121:4).

- He is everywhere (Jeremiah 23:24).

- He possesses knowledge that is limitless
  (Psalm 147:4–5, Psalm 94:9–11, Psalm 139).

- He is consistent with His own goodness
  (2 Timothy 2:13, Hosea 11:9, Isaiah 49:15).

who God is

faithful

"God is faithful, through whom you were called into fellowship with His Son, Jesus Christ our Lord."

—1 Corinthians 1:9 NASB

"So if you find life difficult because you're doing what God said, take it in stride. Trust him. He knows what he's doing, and he'll keep on doing it."

—1 Peter 4:19 THE MESSAGE

"No temptation has seized you except what is common to man. And God is faithful; he will not let you be tempted beyond what you can bear. But when you are tempted, he will also provide a way out so that you can stand up under it."

—1 Corinthians 10:13 NIV

wisdom past and present

"Our God is the great maker of promises. His Word, the Bible, is quite simply a collection of the promises He has made to us. In the beginning God told Adam and Eve, I will send someone who will crush the head of the serpent. A promise. Most of the other promises in the Bible—if you look closely at them—are only a variation on the same theme. They concern Jesus, who would come to be known after all as the 'Promised One.' "

Michael Card, *Immanuel: Reflections on the Life of Christ*

truth tips

Be Faithful—Just as God Is Faithful

▶ **When people look at your life, make sure they see. . .**

   . . .someone constantly dying to Jesus.

   . . .a person of integrity who dares to put his or her life on the line for the gospel.

   . . .a teen with a sincere heart—not a guy or girl hiding behind a mask.

▶ **Be confident.** Never let fear hold you back from befriending an unbeliever.

forgiveness

"Bear with each other and forgive
whatever grievances you may have against one
another. Forgive as the Lord forgave you."

—Colossians 3:13 NIV

"If we confess our sins, He is faithful
and just to forgive us our sins and to
cleanse us from all unrighteousness."

—1 John 1:9 NKJV

"Impressed by their bold belief, he said,
'Friend, I forgive your sins.' "

—Luke 5:20 THE MESSAGE

wisdom past and present

"When Jesus told us to pray for forgiveness of our
debts as we forgive our own debtors, he knew who
would be the one to pay the debt. As he would
hang on the cross he would say, 'It is finished'. . .
the debt is paid!"

Max Lucado, *Grace for the Moment*

truth tips

Forgive as God Forgives

▶ **Accept God's forgiveness.** When you've blown
  it in some way, go to the Lord in prayer.
  Confess your sin, ask for forgiveness, and press
  ahead with the power of the Lord.

▶ **Learn from your mistakes.** It's every
  Christian's responsibility to practice avoiding
  the traps that cause you to stumble.

▶ **Forgive others.** Has somebody wronged
  you? Are you harboring bitterness? Don't
  delay. Go to that person and strive to work
  through the problem. Above all, forgive as
  God forgives.

freedom

"Now the Lord is the Spirit, and where the
Spirit of the Lord is, there is freedom."

—2 Corinthians 3:17 NIV

"Then Jesus turned to the Jews who had
claimed to believe in him. 'If you stick
with this, living out what I tell you, you
are my disciples for sure. Then you will
experience for yourselves the truth, and
the truth will free you.' "

—John 8:31–32 THE MESSAGE

wisdom past and present

"There is freedom in being honest with God that
surpasses the honesty we can have with even our
closest friends. When I pray honestly to God, it
reminds me how much I need His grace and mercy.
If I want to remain in His will and see my life continue to change, I have to make it a priority to
spend time with Him. I don't know how I'd be able
to function without this kind of intimate relationship with Him. Life is extremely challenging. So

many things can distract and corrupt. Being honest with God helps me shed my carefully constructed façade. It eases my burdens and helps me approach my life realistically and hopefully."

Aaron Smith, *Ragamuffin Prayers*

truth tips

A Prayer of Hope, Faith, Freedom

O Lord God, draw me close to You. Protect me in Your arms and let me sense Your power today—the holy, eternal power that can set me free.

Free from the bondage of sin.

Free to live life as a gift of grace.

Free to dream, free to take risks, free to fail.

Free to live in faith and in hope and in love.

O Lord God, let Your truth be the anchor of my life. Restore, repair, renew. . . and heal my life. Amen.

goodness

"Oh, how great is Your goodness,
which You have laid up for those who
fear You, which You have prepared
for those who trust in You in the
presence of the sons of men!"

—Psalm 31:19 NKJV

" 'Why do you ask me about what is
good?' Jesus replied. 'There is only One
who is good. If you want to enter life, obey
the commandments.' "

—Matthew 19:17 NIV

wisdom past and present

"God's truthfulness and trustworthiness, His
unfailing justice and wisdom, His tenderness, for-
bearance, and entire adequacy to all who peni-
tently seek His help, His noble kindness in
offering men the exalted destiny of fellowship
with Him in holiness and love—these things
together make up God's goodness, in the overall
sense of the sum total of His revealed excellences."

J. I. Packer, *Knowing God*

truth tips

An Experiment in Goodness

* Study the quote by J. I. Packer (previous page). Underline God's qualities of goodness, then pray over them. Ask the Lord to develop these qualities in you.

* Are there certain qualities that God wants you to focus on? In other words, are there certain "rough edges" in your life that He wants you to address?

holiness

> "Let them praise Your great
> and awesome name; Holy is He."
>
> —Psalm 99:3 NASB

> "But just as he who called you is holy,
> so be holy in all you do; for it is written:
> 'Be holy, because I am holy.' "
>
> —1 Peter 1:15–16 NIV

reality bytes

Beth, 17, Denver, Colorado

Beth is frustrated. She can't seem to find the right words to explain why the school ski trip is off-limits. What's more, the timing can't be worse. Tina is just now becoming a close friend, and Beth doesn't want to ruin their friendship.

"Look, Tina," Beth says, her eyes darting around the room, "I just can't go. . . Okay?! I'm not being stuck up, I just have other stuff to do."

Beth knows the weekend getaway

will be more of a guy-chasing drinking bash, which goes against her values. Besides, her parents would never let her go on an unsupervised trip.

How on earth do I explain to my friends that holiness is important to me? How do I tell them that obeying Christ is my priority?

truth tips

Choose "The Most Excellent Way"

Holiness. . .

. . .chooses righteousness even when you can get away with sin.

. . .forgets what's behind and presses toward the mark: the high calling of Jesus.

. . .trusts Jesus—even when life doesn't make sense: "Some faced jeers and flogging, while still others were chained and put in prison. They were stoned; they were sawed in two; they were put to death by the sword. They went about in sheepskins and goatskins, destitute, persecuted and mistreated—the world was not worthy of them. They wandered in deserts and mountains, and in caves and holes in the ground. These were all commended for their faith, yet none of them received what had been promised. God had planned something better for us so that only together with us would they be made perfect" (Hebrews 11:36–40 NIV).

holy spirit

"Go out and train everyone you meet,
far and near, in this way of life,
marking them by baptism in the threefold
name: Father, Son, and Holy Spirit.
Then instruct them in the practice of
all I have commanded you. I'll be with
you as you do this, day after day after day,
right up to the end of the age."

—Matthew 28:19–20 THE MESSAGE

"The earth was formless and void, and
darkness was over the surface of the deep,
and the Spirit of God was moving over
the surface of the waters."

—Genesis 1:2 NASB

" 'And I will ask the Father, and he
will give you another Counselor
to be with you forever.' "

—John 14:16 NIV

wisdom past and present

"The Spirit testified to the apostles by revealing to them all truth and inspiring them to communicate it with all truthfulness. Hence the gospel, and hence the New Testament. But the world would have had neither without the Holy Spirit."

J. I. Packer, *Knowing God*

truth tips

The Holy Spirit's Divine Attributes

▶ Everlastingness (Hebrews 9:14)

▶ Omnipresence (Psalm 139:7–10)

▶ Omniscience (1 Corinthians 2:10–11)

▶ Omnipotence (Luke 1:35)

hope

"We have this hope as an anchor
for the soul, firm and secure. It enters
the inner sanctuary behind the curtain,
where Jesus, who went before us,
has entered on our behalf."

—Hebrews 6:19–20 NIV

"For we are saved by hope: but hope
that is seen is not hope: for what a man
seeth, why doth he yet hope for? But
if we hope for that we see not, then
do we with patience wait for it."

—Romans 8:24–25 KJV

wisdom past and present

"It is not Jesus' death and his over-hasty burial
that offers us real meaning. The real glory of
Christianity is its Easter splendor. The cross sym-
bolizes only his dying, but the Resurrection of
God's offering is life."

Calvin Miller, *Once Upon a Tree*

truth tips

Insight on Hope

▶ **Genesis 3 chronicles the beginning of misery**—and hope. The story moves from sin and evil to shame and cover-up, broken fellowship, erected barriers, attack on God, and flight from God.

▶ **Yet the story of The Fall is also one of grace**—God's grace—and hope. It's the hope that began when God broke our unholy alliance with the devil and put hostility between him and us. Misery is still with us. But the time is getting shorter and the hope is getting brighter.

love

"And so we know and rely on the love God has for us. God is love. Whoever lives in love lives in God, and God in him."

—1 John 4:16 NIV

"Love is patient, love is kind and is not jealous; love does not brag and is not arrogant, does not act unbecomingly; it does not seek its own, is not provoked, does not take into account a wrong suffered, does not rejoice in unrighteousness, but rejoices with the truth; bears all things, believes all things, hopes all things, endures all things."

—1 Corinthians 13:4–7 NASB

"Keep yourself in God's love as you wait for the mercy of our Lord Jesus Christ to bring you to eternal life."

—Jude 21 NIV

"Some of us are so afraid that God's not going to look at us, so we're out there doing all sorts of things to get God to take notice. But folks, God notices you. The fact is, He can't take His eyes off of you. However badly you think of yourself, God is crazy about you. God is in love with you. Some of us even fear that someday we'll do something so bad that He won't notice [us] anymore. Well, let me tell you, God loves us completely. And He knew us at our worst before He ever began to love us at all. And in the love of God there are no degrees; there is only love."

Rich Mullins, *Rich Mullins: An Arrow Pointing to Heaven*

truth tips

How to Experience Supernatural Love

▶ **Accept God's love.** We've all heard that God loves us. And we know that God allowed His Son, Jesus Christ, to die on a cross and pay the penalty of our sin—which demonstrate the extent of His love. Then why don't we act as if this is the most incredible news we've ever heard? If God—the One who created us—says we are worthy of His love, why do we pursue what our culture thinks is cool in order to feel good about ourselves?

▶ **Love as God loves.** Need some ideas? Try this: Step out of your clique and get to know someone you normally wouldn't hang out with: the loner in the back of the class, the kid everyone picks on; pray with a hurting friend; send your parents on a date—and pay for it; volunteer to shovel snow from your neighbor's driveway.

merciful

"(For the LORD thy God is a merciful God;) he will not forsake thee, neither destroy thee, nor forget the covenant of thy fathers which he sware unto them."

—Deuteronomy 4:31 KJV

"Be merciful, just as your Father is merciful."

—Luke 6:36 NIV

"But God, being rich in mercy, because of His great love with which He loved us, even when we were dead in our transgressions, made us alive together with Christ (by grace you have been saved)."

—Ephesians 2:4–5 NASB

wisdom past and present

"Mercy is a gift. It is underserved. Punishment and consequences are sin's just reward, but the merciful person does not demand justice for the guilty person. If it were not for God's mercy, we all would have faced His terrible judgment long ago. . . . But rather than letting us bear the full punishment for our sin, God demonstrated His mercy when He paid the penalty for our sin Himself."

Henry T. Blackaby, *Experiencing God Day-By-Day*

truth tips

Some Thoughts About Showing Mercy

- The next time you're tempted to point out the injustices you've had to endure from others, consider the mercy God has graciously bestowed on you.

- Are you finding it difficult to forgive others? Study Nehemiah 9:17 and meditate on God's mercy for us.

- Understand that Jesus commands His followers to show the same mercy to others that God has given them.

who God is

miracles

"You are the God who performs
miracles; you display your power
among the peoples."

—Psalm 77:14 NIV

" 'But so that you may know that the Son
of Man has authority on earth to forgive
sins'—then He said to the paralytic,
'Get up, pick up your bed and go home.'
And he got up and went home."

—Matthew 9:6–7 NASB

"Believe Me that I am in the Father and
the Father in Me, or else believe Me
for the sake of the works themselves."

—John 14:11 NKJV

wisdom past and present

"Miracles are not interruptions of laws, which
must then either be denied by worried intellectu-
als or defended by anxious apologists; they are
expressions of freedom enjoyed by the children of

a wise and exuberant Father. We do not solve these things with rigorous exegesis of the biblical text or with controlled experiments in a laboratory; we *pray* them and in praying enter into dimensions of personal freedom in the universe."

Eugene H. Peterson, Earth & Altar

truth tips

Consider Some of God's Miracles

▶ He created the universe.

▶ He parted the waters of the Red Sea.

▶ He raised His Son from the dead.

▶ He gives believers a new spiritual life.

patience

"I know that You can do all things, and that
no purpose of Yours can be thwarted."

—Job 42:2 NASB

"Be completely humble and gentle; be
patient, bearing with one another in love."

—Ephesians 4:2 NIV

"Be still, and know that I am God;
I will be exalted among the nations,
I will be exalted in the earth!"

—Psalm 46:10 NKJV

"Rest in the LORD, and wait
patiently for Him."

—Psalm 37:7 NKJV

wisdom past and present

"We need to just stop and try to see what's off in the distance. To refocus our lives. To let God rescue us. What's waiting for us out there for each of us is the love of God."

Jimmy Abegg, *Ragamuffin Prayers*

truth tips

Nurturing Patience—Three Questions to Ask

- Is my faith, like my life, in the "fast lane"?

- Am I settling for "McFaith" when God is calling me to slow down and take time to savor my relationship with Him?

- Is my lack of patience hindering my spiritual growth?

peace

"And the peace of God, which transcends
all understanding, will guard your hearts
and your minds in Christ Jesus."

—Philippians 4:7 NIV

"For He Himself is our peace, who
made both groups into one and broke
down the barrier of the dividing wall."

—Ephesians 2:14 NASB

"For unto us a Child is born, unto us a Son
is given; and the government will be upon
His shoulder. And His name will be called
Wonderful, Counselor, Mighty God,
Everlasting Father, Prince of Peace."

—Isaiah 9:6 NKJV

wisdom past and present

"Finally I pray the prayer that is in the last book
of the Bible: 'Lord Jesus, come quickly.' There is
so much still to be done in the world, so much

pain and hurt and injustice to be healed and set right. And only the coming of His kingdom will really bring us peace."

Michael W. Smith, *Ragamuffin Prayers*

truth tips

Consider the "Peace Child"

▮ Because God desires peace, He sent His "peace child"—Jesus Christ—to save humanity.

▮ Christ's death on the cross is God's guarantee to all humankind of the sincerity of His offer for peace.

▮ God wants you to break down the wall of hostility between you and your Savior.

who God is

righteous

> "Glorious and majestic are his deeds,
> and his righteousness endures forever."
>
> —Psalm 111:3 NIV

> "These are the records of the generations of
> Noah. Noah was a righteous man, blameless
> in his time; Noah walked with God."
>
> —Genesis 6:9 NASB

reality bytes

Helping the Homeless in Canada

A church youth group from Colorado Springs had been picking up trash all afternoon around downtown Calgary, Alberta. (The group was participating in a summer mission trip.) As soon as Brian, fifteen, returned to the Mustard Seed (an inner-city mission that helps homeless and drug-addicted people get off the streets), he and his friends were asked to help prepare dinner in the kitchen.

After Brian was done serving meals,

he went outside and talked to the homeless. "You wouldn't think they would be friendly or want to talk," he says. "But most love to talk. All you have to do is open up to them."

And that's exactly what he did. He went to people and asked them how they were or how their meal was. Once he got that far, the conversations took off. One homeless man said that he had lost everything following an accident. He was working as a lumberjack when a tree hit him in the side of the face, causing him to go deaf in one ear.

Brian promised to pray for things to get better for the man. "I don't think he was a Christian," Brian says, "but he still seemed touched by what I said." This conversation showed Brian that it isn't hard to witness to someone. Just listening to them or telling them you will pray can make a huge difference. Above all, Brian discovered that a righteous Christian walk begins with a compassionate heart. "God has called us to care," Brian says. "He wants us to follow His example in word and deed. He wants the world to see a difference in us."

Breakaway magazine

truth tips

Two Keys to a Righteous Walk

▶ **Seek consistency.** Be a promise keeper—the trustworthy guy or girl whom others can count on.
Holiness is lived in secret and in public.

▶ **Follow the Bible's instructions on how to
live:** "Be imitators of God, therefore, as
dearly loved children and live a life of love,
just as Christ loved us and gave himself up for
us as a fragrant offering and sacrifice to God"
(Ephesians 5:1–2 NIV).

Savior

"For whoever desires to save his life
will lose it, but whoever loses his life
for My sake will save it."

—Luke 9:24 NKJV

"Today in the town of David a Savior has
been born to you; he is Christ the Lord."

—Luke 2:11 NIV

"For God so loved the world,
that he gave his only begotten Son,
that whosoever believeth in him should
not perish, but have everlasting life.
For God sent not his Son into the world
to condemn the world; but that the
world through him might be saved."

—John 3:16–17 KJV

reality bytes

Josh, 16, New Carlisle, Ohio

Living as an authentic Christian means
always being conscious of others' feelings,

never putting others down, and not worrying so much about being cool or fitting in with the crowd. Above all, true Christians must have the guts to stand up for their beliefs. And the core truth that every Christian believes is that Jesus Christ is our Lord and Savior. He is the only one who forgives sin and offers eternal life with God.

truth tips

How to Know Jesus Personally

- Agree that your SIN keeps you from having a personal relationship with God. (See Romans 3:23.)

- Believe that JESUS CHRIST died and rose again so that your sins could be forgiven. (See 1 Peter 3:18.)

- Accept God's gift of GRACE. You must also trust Jesus to be your Savior and to forgive you of your sins. (See John 1:12.)

- Understand that you have the promise of eternal life with Him and a CROWN OF RIGHTEOUSNESS! (See 1 John 5:13.)

- Trust Jesus and begin a NEW LIFE in Him! You

can grow in His love, peace, strength, and knowledge. Begin your great adventure now by letting Him guide every step you take. (See 2 Peter 3:18.)

▶ Pray: "Lord Jesus, I agree that I am a sinner who is separated from God. And I know that You have forgiven my sins and offer me the gift of eternal life. I accept this awesome gift. Come into my life right now, fill me with your Holy Spirit, and cleanse me. Make me the person you want me to be. I commit my life to You right now. From this day forward, I give You control. I now live for You. Amen."

Son of God

"They all shouted, 'Then you claim you
are the Son of God?' And He replied,
'You are right in saying that I am.' "

—Luke 22:70 NLT

"And Simon Peter answered and said, Thou
art the Christ, the Son of the living God."

—Matthew 16:16 KJV

"And Jesus, when he was baptized, went up
straightway out of the water: and, lo, the
heavens were opened unto him, and he saw
the Spirit of God descending like a dove,
and lighting upon him: And lo a voice from
heaven, saying, This is my beloved Son,
in whom I am well pleased."

—Matthew 3:16–17 KJV

wisdom past and present

"Don't listen to the fatalistic viewpoints invading
the world today. Don't seek to escape from life's
struggles or believe that you can find peace apart
from God. The truth is, when I was a young
Christian, I had all my little answers. Now I have

only the essential answers and many more questions. I learned firsthand that hope can be found in a committed relationship with Jesus Christ. God loves you more than you can ever image and wants to accomplish incredible things through you—if you let Him."

Phil Keaggy, *Faith That Breathes*

truth tips

Three Truths About the Son of God

- **No beauty.** This is how Isaiah 53:2 describes Christ. Yet if He had no beauty, why do you suppose so many people were attracted to Him? Answer: Christ's beauty was internal. His heart emanated unlimited love. The peace in His eyes drew crowds. The joy of His smile was contagious.

- **No popularity.** The Bible also describes Jesus as one who made himself nothing, taking the very nature of a servant, being made in human likeness (Philippians 2:7 NIV).

- **No sin.** The Bible stamps the words "no sin" on the person of Christ three times. (See 2 Corinthians 5:21, 1 Peter 2:22, 1 John 3:5.)

strength

"I can do all things through
Christ which strengtheneth me."

—Philippians 4:13 KJV

"If anyone speaks, he should do it as one
speaking the very words of God. If anyone
serves, he should do it with the strength God
provides, so that in all things God may be
praised through Jesus Christ. To him be the
glory and the power for ever and ever. Amen."

—1 Peter 4:11 NIV

" 'These words I speak to you are not
incidental additions to your life, homeowner
improvements to your standard of living.
They are foundational words, words to
build your life on. If you work these words
into your life, you are like a smart carpenter
who built his house on solid rock. Rain
poured down, the river flooded, a tornado
hit—but nothing moved that house.
It was fixed to the rock.' "

—Matthew 7:24 THE MESSAGE

wisdom past and present

"Lord, make me an instrument of your peace. Where there is hatred, let me show love. Where there is injury, pardon, where there is doubt, faith, where there is despair, hope, where there is darkness, light, and where there is sadness, joy. O Divine master, grant that I may not so much seek to be consoled as to console; to be understood, as to understand; to be loved, as to love; for it is in giving that we receive—it is in pardoning that we are pardoned; and it is in dying that we are born to eternal life."

St. Francis of Assisi, *Ragamuffin Prayers*

truth tips

Five Ways to Build Spiritual Strength

- Read the Holy Bible daily.
- Memorize Scripture.
- Spend time in prayer with Jesus every day.
- Get plugged into a Bible-believing church.
- Seek out an accountability partner.

trust

"Trust in the LORD with all your heart and do not lean on your own understanding. In all your ways acknowledge Him, and He will make your paths straight."

—Proverbs 3:5–6 NASB

"He trusted in the LORD God of Israel; so that after him was none like him among all the kings of Judah, nor any that were before him. For he clave to the LORD, and departed not from following him, but kept his commandments, which the LORD commanded Moses."

—2 Kings 18:5–6 KJV

"Again, he puts himself in the same family circle when he says, 'Even I live by placing my trust in God.' "

—Hebrews 2:13 THE MESSAGE

"There is a window in your heart through which you can see God. Once upon a time that window was clear. Your view of God was crisp. You could see God as vividly as you could see a gentle valley or hillside. Then, suddenly, the window cracked. A pebble broke the window. A pebble of pain. And suddenly God was not so easy to see. The view that had been so crisp had changed. You were puzzled. God wouldn't allow something like this to happen, would he? When you can't see him, trust him. . . Jesus is closer than you've ever dreamed."

Max Lucado, *Grace for the Moment*

truth tips

Three Reasons to Trust God

- He created you and knows what's best for your life.
- He is absolutely in love with you.
- He wants you to spend eternity with Him.

will of God

"Be imitators of God, therefore, as dearly loved children and live a life of love, just as Christ loved us and gave himself up for us as a fragrant offering and sacrifice to God."

—Ephesians 5:1–2 NIV

"Let every detail in your lives—words, actions, whatever—be done in the name of the Master, Jesus, thanking God the Father every step of the way."

—Colossians 3:17 THE MESSAGE

"But Jesus called for them, saying, 'Permit the children to come to Me, and do not hinder them, for the kingdom of God belongs to such as these.'"

—Luke 18:16 NASB

wisdom past and present

"I have no idea what God is up to in your life and mine, but as He works through His mighty Spirit, we are about to find out! I promise you, it will not be on anybody's chart. You are not going to find a framed copy of it hanging on the wall of some office. God is going to do it in His own way—in startling, unexpected ways—through us as we trust Him and as we pray."

David Jeremiah, *Sanctuary*

truth tips

How to Tune in God's Will

▸ **Strive to fit yourself into what God wants for you rather than what you want for yourself.** Successful people are guided by a clear personal vision of what Christ wants them to accomplish in life—an accurate and precise picture of the work that expresses them best.

▸ **Tune into the spiritual discernment the Holy Spirit provides.** This awareness takes on a "something's not quite right" feeling when God is trying to get you to avoid a course of action—or when danger is lurking nearby. As you grow closer and closer to Him, your entire mind and spirit will become more in tune to God, and you'll begin to hear Him more clearly, just as with any good friend.

◗ Understand that we learn God's will for our lives minute by minute and practice after practice. As we love Him and live in Him, His voice becomes clearer and clearer—and His Word in us grows stronger.

chapter two

what is real

Tuning in Truth

beliefs

"For with God nothing will be impossible."

—Luke 1:37 NKJV

"Jesus said to him, 'I am the way,
the truth, and the life. No one comes
to the Father except through Me.' "

—John 14:6 NKJV

"Jesus said, 'If? There are no "ifs" among
believers. Anything can happen.' "

—Mark 9:23 THE MESSAGE

"And a woman was there who had been
subject to bleeding for twelve years, but
no one could heal her. She came up behind
him and touched the edge of his cloak,
and immediately her bleeding stopped."

—Luke 8:43–44 NIV

wisdom past and present

"We see only in part, yet what we see is enough to give us hope and purpose on our journey. And as we go about our worship here and now, we keep one eye fixed on the horizon, confident that one day the imperfect will disappear and we shall know fully even as we are fully known."

Matt Redman, *The Unquenchable Worshipper*

truth tips

Bible Answers to Agonizing Questions

- **Struggling with sin:** Romans 6:1–14
- **Questioning God's love for you:** Romans 8:31–39
- **Having trouble trusting God:** Psalm 37
- **Trying to get a clue about authentic faith:** Hebrews 11
- **Wondering what heaven is really like:** Revelation 21–22
- **Needing forgiveness:** Psalms 32 and 51

choices

"In him we were also chosen,
having been predestined according to
the plan of him who works out everything
in conformity with the purpose of his will."

—Ephesians 1:11 NIV

"I call heaven and earth to record this
day against you, that I have set before
you life and death, blessing and cursing:
therefore choose life, that both thou
and thy seed may live."

—Deuteronomy 30:19 KJV

"This God is our God for ever and ever;
he will be our guide even to the end."

Psalm 48:14 NIV

wisdom past and present

"Destiny is not a matter of chance, it is a matter of choice; it is not a thing to be waited for, it is a thing to be achieved."

William Jennings Bryan, *Life by Design*

truth tips

How to Choose Wisely

- The fact is, you—and only you—are responsible for your actions. Making the right choices and dealing with the wrong ones, is something you'll have to shoulder all by yourself.

- Will you choose to bend the rules from time to time (knowing that you can), or will you commit to an unshakable faith in Christ? NOW is the time to decide. Like it or not, the days ahead will be filled with all kinds of temptations.

commitment

"But let your 'Yes' be 'Yes' and
your 'No,' 'No.' For whatever is
more than these is from the evil one."

—Matthew 5:37 NKJV

"Commit thy way unto the LORD; trust also
in him; and he shall bring it to pass."

—Psalm 37:5 KJV

"Keep your eyes open, hold tight to
your convictions, give it all you've got,
be resolute, and love without stopping."

—1 Corinthians 16:13–14 THE MESSAGE

wisdom past and present

"I long to accomplish a great and noble task; but it
is my chief duty and joy to accomplish humble tasks
as though they were great and noble. The world is
moved along, not only by the mighty shoves of its
heroes, but also by the aggregate of the tiny pushes
of each honest worker."

Helen Keller, *Your Bridge to a Better Future*

truth tips

Iron-Willed Commitment: Do You Have It?

▶ **Know Whom to trust.** Best-selling author
Max Lucado has a simple strategy for trusting
God. In his book, *He Still Moves Stones,* Max
writes: "Take Jesus at His word. Learn that
when He says something, it happens. When
He says we're forgiven, let's unload the guilt.
When He says we're valuable, let's believe
Him. When He says we're provided for, let's
stop worrying."

Max Lucado, *He Still Moves Stones*

▶ **Know that following Christ is not a passing
fad.** It's a step-by-step, day-by-day commitment. And like any relationship, it requires
your time and devotion in order for it to
grow. "Test everything. Hold on to the good.
Avoid every kind of evil" (1 Thessalonians
5:21–22 NIV).

death

"For the wages of sin is death,
but the gift of God is eternal life
in Christ Jesus our Lord."

—Romans 6:23 NIV

"For since by man came death,
by Man also came the resurrection
of the dead. For as in Adam all die,
even so in Christ all shall be made alive."

—1 Corinthians 15:21–22 NKJV

"For you were once darkness,
but now you are light in the Lord.
Walk as children of light."

—Ephesians 5:8 NKJV

wisdom past and present

"Science tells us that nothing in nature, not even in the tiniest particle, can disappear without a trace. Nature does not know extinction. All it knows is transformation. Now if God applies this fundamental principle of indestructibility to the most minute and insignificant parts of His universe, does it not make sense to assume that He applies it also to the human soul? I think it does. And everything science has taught me and continues to teach me strengthens my belief in the continuity of our spiritual existence after death. Nothing disappears without a trace."

Wernher Von Braun,
"Tried and Transfigured," *Reader's Digest*

truth tips

The Deadly Truth

None of us is immortal. The truth is, scientists will never find a cure for death. Mankind will never escape it (on our own, that is). Some day, whether by accident or illness or old age, each one of us will die. (Unless the Lord returns first!)

Death stings. It's an enemy, not a friend— both of God and of man. Worst of all, death is the ultimate bad day for those who haven't accepted Christ as their Savior.

eternity

"For the wages of sin is death;
but the gift of God is eternal life
through Jesus Christ our Lord."

—Romans 6:23 KJV

"And this is the record, that God hath
given to us eternal life, and this life is in his
Son. He that hath the Son hath life; and he
that hath not the Son of God hath not life."

—1 John 5:11–12 KJV

"In my Father's house are many rooms;
if it were not so, I would have told you.
I am going there to prepare a place for you."

—John 14:2 NIV

wisdom past and present

"Perhaps the heaviest burden we try to carry is the
burden of mistakes and failures. What do you do
with your failures? Even if you've fallen, even if
you've failed, even if everyone else has rejected
you, Christ will not turn away from you. He came

first and foremost to those who have no hope. He goes to those no one else would go to and says, 'I'll give you eternity.' "

Max Lucado, *Grace for the Moment*

truth tips

How to Have Eternal Eyes

▶ **Know where you're headed.** If you're a Christian, you know that your final heartbeat won't be the mysterious end to life. And when you stand at the graveside of a Christian brother or sister, you know your loss is only temporary. That date when you and other believers meet Jesus face to face will be the ultimate homecoming. It will be the grand beginning to a life that never ends.

▶ **Sharing the Good News is the answer.** God doesn't want anyone to miss out on eternal life with Him. But the bottom line is this: Those who don't have a personal friendship with Jesus—those who don't repent of their sins and accept Christ in their hearts—will not have eternal life with God. That's why it's important to share the Lord's plan of salvation with everyone.

goals

"For I know the plans I have for you,"
declares the Lord, "plans to prosper you
and not to harm you, plans to give
you hope and a future."

—Jeremiah 29:11 NIV

"A thief is only there to steal and kill
and destroy. I came so they can have
real and eternal life, more and better
life than they ever dreamed of."

—John 10:10 THE MESSAGE

wisdom past and present

"This is your life we're talking about—the one for
which you are designed—and where that's concerned, I'm sure you'd agree that honesty and thor-
oughness are necessities. When you have
confidently determined and prioritized your values, you are ready to move to the next step in the
process of building the life you most desire: draft-
ing the blueprints for the future of your dreams."

Todd Duncan, *Life by Design*

truth tips

Get a Grip on Goals

▶ **A concrete goal is one you can put into words.** A vague desire to "be a good Christian" is not very concrete. But "join InterVarsity Christian Fellowship my freshman year" is a solid goal. Goals are most concrete when written down.

▶ **A measurable goal is one that allows you to see progress.** The desire to know the Bible from cover to cover is tough to measure. But "read the New Testament this summer" allows you to mark your progress.

▶ **An attainable goal is one that can reasonably be completed.** "Lead the world to Christ" is both concrete and measurable, but hardly attainable. "Introduce three people to Jesus before I graduate from college" is a goal that meets all three criteria.

grief

"Even though I walk through the valley of
the shadow of death, I will fear no evil, for
you are with me; your rod and your staff,
they comfort me."

—Psalm 23:4 NIV

"When he looked out over the crowds, his
heart broke. So confused and aimless they
were, like sheep with no shepherd."

—Matthew 9:36 THE MESSAGE

"He will wipe every tear from their eyes.
There will be no more death or mourning
or crying or pain, for the old order of things
has passed away."

—Revelation 21:4 NIV

wisdom past and present

"The notes [about grieving] have been about
myself, and about H., and about God. In that
order. The order and the proportions exactly what
they ought not to have been. And I see that I have

nowhere fallen into that mode of thinking about either which we call praising them. Yet that would have been best for me. Praise is the mode of love which always has some element of joy in it. Praise is due order; of Him as the giver, of her as the gift. Don't we in praise somehow enjoy what we praise, however far we are from it? I must do more of this."

C. S. Lewis (when he was
grieving the death of his wife),
A Grief Observed

truth tips

The Six Stages of Grief

According to Dr. Kubler-Ross, as a person copes with a trauma he or she moves through six stages of grief:

- **Denial:** "It didn't really happen."
- **Anger:** "It's not fair!"
- **Bargaining:** "God, if you take away this pain, I promise I'll be a better person."
- **Depression:** "I don't want to talk to anyone or do anything. Just leave me alone."
- **Acceptance:** "It happened and that's that."
- **Hope:** "It's really going to be okay."

> "Let us draw near to God with a
> sincere heart in full assurance of faith,
> having our hearts sprinkled to cleanse
> us from a guilty conscience and having
> our bodies washed with pure water."

—Hebrews 10:22 NIV

> "For the LORD God is a sun and shield;
> The LORD will give grace and glory;
> No good thing will He withhold
> from those who walk uprightly."

—Psalm 84:11 NKJV

reality bytes

Forgiven and Free?

A well-meaning father decided to teach
his thirteen-year-old son a visual lesson
about the consequences of sin. The father
held up a two-by-four. "Notice the three
nails in it?" he asked.

His son nodded.

"I'm going to pull out the nails," the father continued. "There! Now what do you see?"

"Holes," the son responded. "It's a worn two-by-four with three big holes in it."

"Exactly!" the father said. "It's the same way with sin in our lives. We may end up making mistakes that can hurt ourselves and others. And while we may be forgiven by those we've wronged, the holes will always be there. People will never forget what we've done."

A stern expression washed over the father's face as he locked eyes with his son. "So, the next time you're tempted to sin, think about the holes."

Is this really how God works? Are our mistakes like nails in a board that our Creator never forgets? Absolutely not! When we seek Jesus Christ and repent of our sins, we are fully forgiven.

True, we will face consequences for our actions. . .and, true, we may have scars that will take a lifetime to heal. Yet through the power of the Holy Spirit, we are washed clean and set free. . .and are given a new beginning.

How to Let God Cleanse a Guilty Conscience

▶ Count the cost. Here's what the dad described above should have told his son: "The next time you're tempted to sin, think about the holes: the price Jesus paid on the cross. He'll give you the power to resist. He'll set you free from the slavery of sin."

▶ Grasp God's forgiveness. Too many people are convinced that they are just "too bad to be a follower of Christ." Here's the truth: When you blow it, go to the Lord in prayer. Confess your sin; ask for forgiveness. Then press ahead with the hope of Jesus Christ.

▶ Grow from mistakes. It's every Christian's responsibility to practice avoiding the traps that cause them to stumble. Impress upon your heart the message of Philippians 3:12 NIV: "Not that I have already obtained all this, or have already been made perfect, but I press on to take hold of that for which Christ Jesus took hold of me."

heaven

"Thus saith the LORD, the heaven is my throne, and the earth is my footstool: where is the house that ye build unto me? and where is the place of my rest?"

—Isaiah 66:1 KJV

"Now we know that if the earthly tent we live in is destroyed, we have a building from God, an eternal house in heaven, not built by human hands."

—2 Corinthians 5:1 NIV

"In the beginning God created the heavens and the earth."

—Genesis 1:1 NASB

wisdom past and present

"Of all the blessings of heaven, one of the greatest will be you! You will be God's magnum opus, his work of art. The angels will gasp. God's work will be completed. At last, you will have a heart like his. You will love with perfect love. You will worship with a radiant face. You'll hear each word God speaks. Your heart will be pure, your words will be like jewels, your thoughts will be like treasures. You will be just like Jesus. You will, at long last, have a heart like his."

Max Lucado, *Grace for the Moment*

truth tips

The Only Path to Heaven: Two Truths

▶ **Don't try to earn your way into heaven.** It just CAN'T be done. NOTHING you do, including "good" works, can protect you from the burning flame of God's holiness. *"All our righteous acts are like filthy rags; we all shrivel up like a leaf, and like the wind our sins sweep us away"* (Isaiah 64:6 NIV).

▶ **Trust Christ and what He accomplished by His death and resurrection.** This is the one true path to eternity.

hell

"But the subjects of the kingdom will be thrown outside, into the darkness, where there will be weeping and gnashing of teeth."

—Matthew 8:12 NIV

"For if God did not spare angels when they sinned, but sent them to hell, putting them into gloomy dungeons to be held for judgment. . ."

—2 Peter 2:4 NIV

wisdom past and present

"Eons ago, in Hell's court, Satan decreed a law that, as prince of the world, all living souls were his subjects. God's supreme court killed that law of sin. It died because Satan could not enforce it anymore. God declared it unconstitutional and substituted His own law—the law of the spirit— giving Him all rights to the believer's body."

David Wilkerson, *Victory Over Sin and Self*

What You Need to Know About Hell

▶ It is a real place.

▶ It is eternal separation from God.

▶ It is a place that God gives you a way to avoid.

▶ It is reality for those who do not trust
   the Savior.

▶ It is NOT reality for Christians: people who
   have committed their lives to Jesus Christ.

life

"Jesus said to her, 'I am the resurrection and the life. He who believes in me will live, even though he dies; and whoever lives and believes in me will never die. Do you believe this?' "

—John 11:25–26 NIV

"Then the LORD God formed man of dust from the ground, and breathed into his nostrils the breath of life; and man became a living being."

—Genesis 2:7 NASB

reality bytes

Life on the Edge:

"I'm sick of being a wimpy Christian," fifteen-year-old Jason confesses to his buddies in discipleship group. "I act one way at church and around you guys, then another way with my friends at school. It's like...I don't even know who I am at times."

Jason's comments strike a nerve with the four other boys lounging on my living room floor. Chris and Andy, both sixteen, nod their heads in agreement, and fourteen-year-old Brian—who has been busy all evening stuffing his face with chips—perks up, too.

"I know God doesn't like it when I act this way," Jason continues. "And I know I need to give up a few bad friendships so I can grow stronger as a Christian. But it's really hard."

Suddenly, a serious expression washes across Brian's face. "I'm with you, Jason," he says. "I've been a wimp with my faith. I've got some stuff to change in my life, too."

Just as the youth leader is about to jump in with a few words of encouragement, Chad—one of the older guys in the group—speaks up. "You're on the right track," the seventeen-year-old says. "Lose those friendships that are pulling you down. That's what I had to do.

"I used to care more about popularity than my faith," Chad continues. "Then one day I thought to myself, *It's stupid to follow* the crowd at school. I'm a Christian. I'm different. . .and that's okay."

Jason sits up. "I've got it," he says with a grin. "Let's make a pact for purity. Let's help each other commit to a deeper faith in God."

The youth leader sits back and watches with amazement. *These guys are spurring each other to a deeper walk with Christ,* he thinks to himself. *These boys are growing up!*

truth tips

Can't-Miss Life Lessons

▶ The crucified Jesus really had risen from the dead and truly is the Savior of all.

▶ The wages of sin is death, but Jesus paid that price for humankind. Therefore, salvation is gained only through a relationship with Jesus—not by following the rigid laws of the Pharisees. . .or any other worldly philosophy.

▶ Christians must never be ashamed of the Good News of the gospel and must boldly spread it throughout the world—regardless of bitter opposition.

"Hear counsel, and receive instruction, that
thou mayest be wise in thy latter end."

—Proverbs 19:20 KJV

"You shall walk after the LORD your God
and fear Him, and keep His commandments and obey His voice; you shall serve
Him and hold fast to Him."

—Deuteronomy 13:4 NKJV

" 'Because a loveless world,' said Jesus,
'is a sightless world. If anyone loves me,
he will carefully keep my word and my
Father will love him—we'll move right
into the neighborhood!' "

—John 14:23 THE MESSAGE

wisdom past and present

"To pray, 'Thy will be done' is to seek the heart of
God. The word *will* means 'strong desire'. . .[So]
what is his heart? His passion? He wants you to
know it. . . . God is not the God of confusion,

and wherever he sees sincere seekers with confused hearts, you can bet your sweet December that he will do whatever it takes to help them see his will."

Max Lucado, Grace for the Moment

truth tips

How to "Dis" Disobedience

▶ **Understand that living for Christ is expensive— it costs everything!** (Especially stuff like trust, commitment, and 100% rock-solid obedience to Him.) The choice is yours. Will you follow the crowd and conform to the world, or will you commit yourself to standing strong for God? It all starts with the first step: desire to follow Christ.

▶ **Remove the roadblocks. . .this is the next crucial step.** Ask Jesus to search your heart and to help you pinpoint specific sins that are holding you back from an obedient relationship with Him. After praying, take out a notebook and a pen. On the top left-hand side of one page write: "Things I Must Get Right With God." Then list all the stuff you need to confess to the Lord. Ask God to do a deep work in your soul. Allow Him to examine every area of your life. (Example: Perhaps you have a problem with envy or a bad temper. Confess these sins to God.)

▶ **Do business with the Lord without delay.** Commit to being obedient to Him in every area of your life. While the cost is expensive, the reward is unreal: "This is the confidence we have in approaching God: that if we ask anything according to his will, he hears us. And if we know that he hears us—whatever we ask—we know that we have what we asked of him" (1 John 5:14–15 NIV).

prayer

"Therefore I say to you, whatever things you ask when you pray, believe that you receive them, and you will have them."

—Mark 11:24 NKJV

"The LORD has heard my supplication, the LORD receives my prayer."

—Psalm 6:9 NASB

"We are ambassadors for Christ, as though God did beseech you by us: we pray for you in Christ's stead, be ye reconciled to God. For he hath made him to be sin for us, who knew no sin; that we might be made the righteousness of God in him."

—2 Corinthians 5:20-21 KJV

"The effectual fervent prayer of a righteous man availeth much."

—James 5:16 KJV

"God's supernatural help is promised to those who thrash about in the deep, dark womb of evil, struggling to be free. And the surest sign that new life is springing up in the sinner is the urgency to cry out. All newborn children cry as soon as they come to life. Those who cry are really on the verge of a new life. The first step toward ending your inner struggle is to learn how to cry."

David Wilkerson, *Victory Over Sin and Self*

truth tips

Consider These Thoughts About Prayer

▶ You don't need to be in church.

▶ You don't need to kneel.

▶ You don't need to do anything with your hands.

▶ You don't even have to raise your voice.

salvation

"I am the gate; whoever enters
through me will saved."

—John 10:9 NIV

"For God so loved the world that He
gave His only begotten Son, that whoever
believes in Him should not perish but
have everlasting life. For God did not
send His Son into the world to condemn
the world, but that the world through
Him might be saved."

—John 3:16–17 NKJV

"When Christ, who is our life,
is revealed, then you also will be
revealed with Him in glory."

—Colossians 3:4 NASB

widsom past and present

"Costly grace is the gospel, which must be sought
again and again, the gift that must be asked for, the
door at which a man must knock. Such grace is

costly because it calls us to follow, and it is grace because it calls us to follow Jesus Christ. It is costly because it costs a man his life, and it is grace because it gives a man the only true life. It is costly because it condemns sin, and grace because it justifies the sinner. Above all, it is costly because it cost God the life of his Son: 'ye were bought at a price,' and what has cost God much cannot be cheap for us. Above all, it is grace because God did not reckon his Son too dear a price to pay for our life, but delivered him up for us. Costly grace is the Incarnation of God."

Dietrich Bonhoeffer, *The Cost of Discipleship*

i believe

truth tips

Salvation is a Free Gift

▶ **Jesus paid the price for sin.** For reasons not entirely clear, God won't just wipe away our sins without a sacrificial death. Someone had to die for us, and the only death God could accept on our behalf was the death of His sinless Son—Jesus.

▶ **Jesus died for YOU!** "For Christ died for sins once and for all, the righteous for the unrighteous, to bring you to God" (1 Peter 3:18 NIV).

- **Through Jesus Christ, your sins are completely forgiven.** Your slate is clean. You have a spotless record with Him and can now have eternal fellowship with God.

- **Jesus offers YOU eternal life!** "For God so loved the world that he gave his one and only Son, that whoever believes in him shall not perish but have eternal life" (John 3:16 NIV).

satan

> "Keep a cool head. Stay alert. The Devil is poised to pounce, and would like nothing better than to catch you napping."
>
> —1 Peter 5:8 THE MESSAGE

> "And a great dragon was thrown down, the serpent of old who is called the devil and Satan, who deceives the whole world; he was thrown down to the earth, and his angels were thrown down with him."
>
> —Revelation 12:9 NASB

wisdom past and present

"Satan is not portrayed as a mere metaphor or symbol of evil in Scripture; he is a created being who entices towards evil. His very name means 'accuser,' and it aptly describes him. As a creature, he is limited, finite, and constrained by his Creator. He is not [a] sovereign, all-powerful being. . . . Put simply: Satan is not equal to God. Christianity is not a dualistic religion, a faith in which two opposing but equal powers struggle for control. Even so, many Christians live as though Satan were as powerful as God. Nothing could be further from the truth! . . . Because God is sovereign Satan does not stand a chance."

A. Scott Moreau, *Essentials of Spiritual Warfare*

truth tips

Two Truths About the Enemy

▶ Some of your friends may call Satan stuff a big joke. Others may be lured into the occult, thinking it's good for a few thrills. What do you believe? Is there a spiritual battle raging in the world today? Is Satan for real? Just look at all the messed up teens at school or all the broken families that live in your town. The devil is real. He's our enemy, and he's playing for keeps. He and his troops are viciously attacking the kingdom of God. His target: our souls.

▶ Here's the good news: Jesus is a Christian's ultimate ally—his defender. But ask yourself an important question: *Do I have a personal, active relationship with Jesus. . .or am I just going through the motions?*

security

"You shall keep them, O LORD,
You shall preserve them from this
generation forever."

—Psalm 12:7 NKJV

" 'Before I formed you in the womb I knew
you; before you were born I sanctified you;
I ordained you a prophet to the nations.' "

—Jeremiah 1:5 NKJV

"Don't be obsessed with getting more material things. Be relaxed with what you have.
Since God assured us, 'I'll never let you
down, never walk off and leave you. . .' "

—Hebrews 13:5 THE MESSAGE

wisdom past and present

"As Jesus' cry of loneliness faded into stillness,
there was nothing but the whisper of afternoon
breeze and the scream of the carrion eagles, cir-
cling in the sickly sky above the tree. But Jesus'
tormentors were wrong in their conclusions.

There is always a time when the silence ends. There is always a time when God answers evil!"

Calvin Miller, *Once Upon a Tree*

truth tips

Three Reasons to Feel Secure

▶ **SECURITY TRUTH #1:** Jesus Christ forgives our sin and frees us from bondage and eternal death. Somehow, as we give Him control of our lives and spend time with Him, the old desires and enslavements just sort of fade away.

▶ **SECURITY TRUTH #2:** Want freedom through Christ instead of judgment? The key is to stand before Him with your arms already reaching out for help—not folded across our chests in smug piety.

▶ **SECURITY TRUTH #3:** Not only does Jesus forgive us when we sin, but He actually gives us the power to obey Him and to pursue holiness. Accept that power.

sin

"Let no one say when he is tempted, 'I am being tempted by God'; for God cannot be tempted by evil, and He Himself does not tempt anyone."

— James 1:13 NASB

"We know that when Jesus was raised from the dead it was a signal of the end of death-as-the-end. Never again will death have the last word. When Jesus died, he took sin down with him, but alive he brings God down to us."

—Romans 6:11 THE MESSAGE

wisdom past and present

"The most important thing I can say to a believer who is sincerely battling a secret sin is: Keep your momentum! No one has ever drowned when swimming upstream toward Christ. No one is left bleeding by the wayside if he is wounded in his struggle to be free."

David Wilkerson, *Victory Over Sin and Self*

truth tips

How to Defeat Sin

▶ **Don't drown in sin.** Understand three truths. (1) You can't swim against the tide of God and survive. But you can come to the surface and cry out, "Abba, Father," and He'll set you on the right course. (2) Not one person on this planet is outside the reach of God's love. (3) Even if you can't begin to fathom the depth of your sin—Jesus understands. And He forgives you.

▶ **Restore your relationship:** Admit the mistakes you've made. Take a long, honest look at sin in your life, then tell Jesus Christ that you're sorry (make sure you mean it). Once you've confessed the sin and asked Him to help you change (called repentance), you can stop flogging yourself. You're totally forgiven. Now with your relationship fully restored with God, you can take steps toward growth and change. (The Holy Spirit will help you.)

truth

" 'These are the things you are to do:
Speak the truth to each other, and render
true and sound judgment in your courts;
do not plot evil against your neighbor,
and do not love to swear falsely.
I hate all this,' declares the LORD."

—Zechariah 8:16–17 NIV

"In the beginning was the Word,
and the Word was with God,
and the Word was God."

—John 1:1 NASB

wisdom past and present

"The day when Christians should meekly apologize is over—they can get the world's attention not by trying to please, but by boldly declaring the truth of divine revelation. They can make themselves heard not by compromise, but by taking the affirmative and sturdily declaring, 'Thus saith the Lord.' "

A.W. Tozer, *Tozer on Christian Leadership*

truth tips

How to Tune in Truth

▸ **Desire truth.** While most Christian teens understand that their lives could—and SHOULD—be a reflection of Jesus Christ, they allow peer fear to get in the way. Jesus said, " 'Then you will know the truth, and the truth will set you free' " (John 8:32 NIV). Are you among the many who haven't allowed the truth to set them free? If so, it's time for a change.

▸ **Choose truth.** If you're ready to allow God to speak words of truth to you, it's time to do something radical. Sit down in the quietness of your room (no stereo, please), and let the invisible God speak the truth to you through His Word. The Bible isn't only for parents and pastors; it's for YOU! The only way you can *believe* the truth is to *know* the truth.

wisdom

"But if any of you lacks wisdom,
let him ask of God, who gives to all
generously and without reproach,
and it will be given to him."

—James 1:5 NASB

"For the LORD gives wisdom; from His
mouth come knowledge and understanding."

—Proverbs 2:6 NKJV

wisdom past and present

"When the Bible talks about wisdom, it means
more than scoring a 1400 on the SAT. Much
more. Biblical wisdom involves the skills of walking right with God and understanding how to
apply His truth to your life."

Bruce H. Wilkinson, *Youthwalk Again*

truth tips

The Way of Wisdom

- Disconnect from the world's lies and stand firmly in God's truth. "There is a way that seems right to a man, but in the end it leads to death" (Proverbs 14:12 NIV).

- Evaluate your weak points, then take action. "Let us throw off everything that hinders. . . and let us run with perseverance the race marked out for us" (Hebrews 12:1 NIV).

worship

"O come, let us worship and bow down:
let us kneel before the LORD our maker."

—Psalm 95:6 KJV

"Jesus said, 'Love the Lord your God
with all your passion and prayer and
intelligence.' This is the most important,
the first on any list."

—Matthew 22:37–38 THE MESSAGE

wisdom past and present

"Sometimes it comes down to a simple choice.
We may be hard-pressed on every side, weary and
not able to sense God. But then a choice faces
us—to fix our eyes on the circumstances or to
cling to God and choose to worship Him, even
when it hurts. The heart of God loves the offerings of a persevering worshipper. Though overwhelmed by many troubles, they are even more
overwhelmed by the beauty of God."

Matt Redman, *The Unquenchable Worshipper*

truth tips

Get Wired for Worship

As you worship God, you SHOULD. . .

> . . .give Him your praise and glory.

> . . .give Him your thanks.

> . . .give Him your whole heart.

As you worship God, you SHOULDN'T. . .

> . . .go through the motions of an
> empty ritual.

> . . .approach Him with wrong
> motives, using your praise as a
> means of getting something.

> . . .treat this special time as an option
> in your life.

chapter three

i feel like

Dealing with Your Emotions

acceptance

> "As for those who were considered important in the church, their reputation doesn't concern me. God isn't impressed with mere appearances, and neither am I."
>
> —Galatians 2:6 THE MESSAGE

> " 'Do not judge so that you will not be judged. For in the way you judge, you will be judged; and by your standard of measure, it will be measured to you.' "
>
> —Matthew 7:1–2 NASB

> "Therefore, accept one another, just as Christ also accepted us to the glory of God."
>
> —Romans 15:7 NASB

reality bytes

Chris, 14, Seattle, Washington

You could say that I suffer from serious low self-esteem. But I recently made a friend— someone who actually accepts me and sees in me what other people seem to miss. His name is Jesus Christ. And through Him, I've learned that if I pray, read the Bible, and seek God with all my heart, then He will see me through life's problems. He will even help me to like myself. You see, after being told for so long what a loser I am, God is helping me see that I'm a real winner—and that's all that matters.

truth tips

How to Build Confidence

▶ **Find at least one true friend.** Now more than ever, you need a buddy you can trust— someone who will stand by you and accept you just as you are. Seek out a strong Christian who shares your values.

▶ **Never try to be someone you're not— or force yourself to do something you can't.** God made you an awesome person just as you are. Stand strong in the strengths and talents He gave you.

▶ **Understand that you're NOT weird because you don't hang out with the popular crowd.** It doesn't matter if you can't play sports very well or if you don't have a perfect body. Every day, when you get up and look in the mirror, repeat these words: "I'm okay."

▶ **Remind yourself that your circumstances will change.** This isn't how things are going to be forever. Your body is changing and so are your abilities. If you don't like yourself right now, don't lose hope. In a few years, you'll find your niche.

anger

> "A gentle answer turns away wrath,
> but a harsh word stirs up anger."
>
> —Proverbs 15:1 NIV

> "Post this at all the intersections, dear
> friends: Lead with your ears, follow up
> with your tongue, and let anger straggle
> along in the rear. God's righteousness
> doesn't grow from human anger."
>
> —James 1:19 THE MESSAGE

wisdom past and present

"Believe it or not, there's a right way and wrong way to get mad. While some people feel it's unchristian to express anger, you may be surprised to find the Bible actually offers guidelines on getting angry the right way. After all, being a Christian doesn't mean life is always great. Like other guys, you flunk tests, spill grape juice on your new white T-shirt, and get into disagreements with your friends. For some clues on handling anger, study Ephesians 4:26."

T. J. Cleary, "Taming Your Temper," *Breakaway* magazine

Threefold Strategy to Getting Angry (the Right Way)

◗ **Sometimes it's okay to be angry.** Get this: Several times during His ministry, Jesus became angry with people or circumstances. Why? On occasion, our Lord spoke angrily in order to show people the true way to God—through himself. Jesus knew what was important enough to get angry about (where people would spend eternity).

◗ **Be angry but do not sin.** Express your anger the right way. Screaming matches and slugfests don't accomplish anything. If something is important enough to get angry about, then it's important enough to try to work out.

◗ **Don't let the sun go down on your anger.** Quickly settle whatever has you angry. If you allow your anger to fester, your circumstances can grow bigger than the Goodyear blimp.

anxiety

" 'Therefore I tell you, do not worry about
your life, what you will eat or drink; or
about your body, what you will wear. Is not
life more important than food, and the
body more important than clothes?' "

—Matthew 6:25 NIV

"Therefore humble yourselves under the
mighty had of God, that He may exalt you
at the proper time, casting all your anxiety
on Him, because He cares for you."

—1 Peter 5:6–7 NASB

" 'Blessed is the man who trusts in the
LORD, whose confidence is in him.' "

—Jeremiah 17:7 NIV

wisdom past and present

"God will not necessarily take your problems
away, but He will carry the load for you. He wants
you to experience His peace, which is beyond
human comprehension. You will never fully

understand how God could give you peace in some of the situations you face, but you do not have to understand it in order to experience it. . . . Scripture says to be anxious for nothing. God's Word clearly indicates that there is nothing you can face that is too difficult, too troubling, or too fearful for God."

Henry T. Blackaby, *Experiencing God Day-By-Day*

truth tips

Pray About Your Anxious Attitude

"Lord God, do whatever it takes to get me on the right path with You. I want peace, not constant worry. I want joy, not nagging jitters. Heal my heart. Make me the person You want me to be. Amen."

arrogance

"Look not every man on his own things,
but every man also on the things of others."

—Philippians 2:4 KJV

"As it is, you boast and brag. All such boast-
ing is evil. Anyone, then, who knows the
good he ought to do and doesn't do it, sins."

—James 4:16 NIV

"For by grace you have been saved through
faith; and that not of yourselves,
it is the gift of God; not as a result of
works, so that no one may boast."

—Ephesians 2:8–9 NASB

wisdom past and present

"Has that break come? All the rest is pious fraud.
The one point to decide is—Will I give up, will I
surrender to Jesus Christ, and make no conditions
whatever as to how the break comes? I must be broken from my self-realization, and immediately that
point is reached, the reality of the supernatural
identification takes place at once, and the witness

of the Spirit of God is unmistakable—'I have been crucified with Christ.' "

Oswald Chambers, *My Utmost for His Highest*

truth tips

How to Put an End to Arrogance

▸ **Strive to be selfless.** Ask "How can I help others?" not "How can others get me what I want?"

▸ **Have frequent "attitude checks."** Are you seeing with Christ's eyes, or is pride clouding your judgment? Are you walking with humility, or is your ego a little too inflated?

▸ **Be an encourager.** Be one of the few who remind their friends of their strengths and abilities.

▸ **Cut back on the cuts!** Don't let a few "friendly" putdowns become a habit. Vow to be different.

▸ **Defend your friends—especially when someone is talking bad behind their backs.** Also, never give in to the gossip game.

▸ **Walk with the Savior.** Above all, point others to the One who will always tell them the truth.

beauty

"I will praise thee; for I am fearfully and wonderfully made: marvellous are thy works; and that my soul knoweth right well."

—Psalm 139:14 KJV

"And God saw every thing that he had made, and, behold, it was very good. And the evening and the morning were the sixth day."

—Genesis 1:31 KJV

"Your adornment must not be merely external—braiding the hair, and wearing gold jewelry, or putting on dresses; but let it be the hidden person of the heart, with the imperishable quality of a gentle and quiet spirit, which is precious in the sight of God."

—1 Peter 3:3–4 NASB

reality bytes

Lisa, 19, Nashville, Tennessee

My generation is bombarded with completely unrealistic images of what the world defines as beauty. Women are pressured to look like the latest supermodel, while guys are expected to look like muscle-bound hunks. Yet the Word of God tells us that inside qualities matter more than outward beauty—qualities like integrity, honor, compassion, humility. As Christians, we need to redefine beauty. Above all, let's build up each other's self-esteem, not tear it down.

truth tips

Three Thoughts About Beauty

▶ Why is it the stuff on the inside that makes the outside truly beautiful?

▶ Why should a Christian's identity be grounded in God? (For a clue, see 1 John 3:1.)

▶ Why are you so valuable to God—regardless of how you look?

boldness

"Now, Lord, consider their threats and enable your servants to speak your word with great boldness."

—Acts 4:29 NIV

"Watch, stand fast in the faith, be brave, be strong. Let all that you do be done with love."

—1 Corinthians 16:13–14 NKJV

wisdom past and present

"Heroes don't faint or flinch when the fingers of fear attempt to pinch their arm or punch their chin or poke them in the eye. They don't try to be bold, they just are. Heroes face disgrace without a trace of regret. They don't fret about what others think. They simply do what they think they should without a second thought. Without fright they accept the stage God has permitted them. And taking their cues from the playwright Himself, heroes act courageously."

Greg Asimakoupoulos, *Heroic Faith*

How to Take Some Bold Steps

▌ **Confident Christians aren't paralyzed by failures, flops, and fumbles.** The Lord wants to transform tremendously flawed individuals into heroes who are fit to accomplish His purpose. Don't let life's blunders get in the way. Instead, let God have His way.

▌ **Confident Christians strive to be their brother's keeper.** "Those of us who are strong and able in the faith need to step in and lend a hand to those who falter, and not just do what is most convenient for us. Strength is for service, not status. Each one of us needs to look after the good of the people around us, asking ourselves, 'How can I help?'" (Romans 15:1–3 THE MESSAGE).

change

"I the LORD do not change. So you,
O descendants of Jacob, are not destroyed."

—Malachi 3:6 NIV

"Nothing between us and God, our faces
shining with the brightness of his face.
And so we are transfigured much like the
Messiah, our lives gradually becoming
brighter and more beautiful as God enters
our lives and we become like him."

—2 Corinthians 3:18 THE MESSAGE

"I will give you a new heart and put a new
spirit within you; I will take the heart of
stone out of your flesh and give you a heart
of flesh. I will put My Spirit within you and
cause you to walk in My statutes, and you
will keep My judgments and do them."

—Ezekiel 36:26–27 NKJV

wisdom past and present

"Everything else may change, but Jesus never will.
He's the same yesterday, today, and forever

(Hebrews 13:8). This changing world will one day disappear (2 Peter 3:12), but your Savior holds eternity in His palm. Rest in those unchanging hands."

Manfred Koehler, missionary to Mexico,
"When Change Scares You," *Breakaway* magazine

truth tips

Write Yourself a Letter

Change is on the horizon—whether that means graduation, heading to college or the workplace, or moving to a new town. No doubt, change can be scary. Tackle the anxiety and fear right now by putting down some thoughts in a letter to yourself.

That's right! Write out what being a Christian means to you—how being a new creation affects your behavior and choices and fills you with peace and confidence. Also, list a description of the kind of person Christ wants you to be. (Don't forget to list your core Christian values somewhere in your letter.) Next, put this personal note in an envelope labeled "Open on My First Day of College" (or "The Day of My Big Move"). You'll thank yourself later for taking this step.

depression

"I waited patiently for the LORD;
he turned to me and heard my cry.
He lifted me out of the slimy pit, out of
the mud and mire; he set my feet on a
rock and gave me a firm place to stand."

—Psalm 40:1–2 NIV

"Blessed be God, who has not turned away
my prayer nor His lovingkindness from me."

—Psalm 66:20 NASB

wisdom past and present

"When you're depressed and unhappy and blue,
when nothing is going right and life doesn't seem
to be worth living, just hang tough for a few days.
Your circumstances will change and the sun will
come up again. Sooner or later you'll wake up in
the morning and be glad you're alive."

James Dobson, *Preparing for Adolescence*

truth tips

Deflating Depression

▸ **Talk it out.** Open up to your parents, a youth
leader, or a Christian counselor. Be honest with
them about what you're feeling. Above all,
don't keep it in; that's not fair to you.

▸ **Learn to value your value.** Whenever nega-
tive thoughts and brain graffiti begins to
mess with your mind, stop and remind yourself of two awesome truths: (1) You were
created by God Almighty, the God of the
universe, and if God is for you, who can be
against you? (2) You can do all things through
Christ who gives you strength.

▸ **Pray.** God cares. He will help you through
anything you are facing.

fear

> "Peace I leave with you; my peace
> I give you. I do not give to you
> as the world gives. Do not let your
> hearts be troubled and do not be afraid."
>
> — John 14:27 NIV

> "There is no room in love for fear.
> Well-formed love banishes fear.
> Since fear is crippling, a fearful life—
> fear of death, fear of judgment—
> is one not yet fully formed in love."
>
> —1 John 4:18 THE MESSAGE

wisdom past and present

"Jesus' presence always brought astonishing peace to me no matter how bad the situation I was in. Whenever I was in a prison, He was always there for me. He transformed the jail into a heaven and the burdens became blessings. There are many Christians who do not feel His glorious presence as something real, because for them Jesus only occurs in their minds and not in their hearts. Only when someone surrenders his heart to Jesus can he find Him."

Sundar Singh, missionary to Tibet, *Jesus Freaks*

truth tips

Take the Scare Out of Fear

◗ God is still in control: " 'Fear not, for I have redeemed you; I have summoned you by name; you are mine. When you pass through the waters, I will be with you; and when you pass through the rivers, they will not sweep over you. When you walk through the fire, you will not be burned; the flames will not set you ablaze. For I am the LORD, your God, the Holy One of Israel, your Savior' " (Isaiah 43:1–3 NIV).

◗ God's love drives out fear: "God is love. Whoever lives in love lives in God, and God in him. In this way, love is made complete among us so that we will have confidence on the day of judgment, because in this world we are like him. There is no fear in love. But perfect love drives out fear, because fear has to do with punishment. The one who fears is not made perfect in love" (1 John 4:16–18 NIV).

hypocrisy

"For if anyone is a hearer of the word and not a doer, he is like a man observing his natural face in a mirror; for he observes himself, goes away, and immediately forgets what kind of man he was."

—James 1:23–24 NKJV

" 'Be especially careful when you are trying to be good so that you don't make a performance out of it. It might be good theater, but the God who made you won't be applauding.' "

—Matthew 6:1 THE MESSAGE

reality bytes

Troy, 15, Los Angeles, California

"Stop living a lie, Troy. Your life's out of control. Want to do something worth-while with yourself? Start by giving every-thing to Jesus."

The words echoed through my head, leaving a sickening pain in the pit of my stomach. *My parents are right,* I told myself. *My life is falling apart.* I knew that my world had already slipped over the edge—and that I was tumbling into a deadly pit of drugs, street violence, and "nowhere friend- ships" that had gotten me kicked out of school and in trouble with the law. So I did the unthinkable. I squeezed shut my eyes and began to pray.

"Lord, I don't know how I went from being a good Christian kid to being such a hypocrite. But I've got to make a change. I was stupid to give into drugs, and I was crazy to listen to my friends. But now I'm giving my life to You."

I opened my eyes and felt the peace of God. *For once in my life, I've done some- thing right,* I told myself.

truth tips

Put an End to Phony Faith

▶ **Seek out an accountability partner.** As you talk honestly with another person, you'll probably discover that the things you think are your problems are just symptoms of a deeper heart problem. And God is faithful and willing to help. If you let Him, He'll transform your damaged heart.

▶ **Strive to be real.** Understand that there's no greater witness than a Christian who is open and vulnerable about his or her struggles. On the other hand, believers who act as if they don't have problems are the biggest stumbling blocks to unbelieving family and friends.

▶ **Don't harbor secrets.** Never believe the lie that you can ever say something, do something, go somewhere, or think things that God—and possibly others—won't know about. People who believe in secrets are people who get into trouble.

jealousy

"But the fruit of the Spirit is love, joy, peace, patience, kindness, goodness, faithfulness, gentleness and self-control. Against such things there is no law."

—Galatians 5:22–23 NIV

"Let nothing be done through selfish ambition or conceit, but in lowliness of mind let each esteem others better than himself."

—Philippians 2:3 NKJV

"Let your conversation be without covetousness; and be content with such things as ye have: for he hath said, I will never leave thee, nor forsake thee."

Hebrews 13:5 KJV

wisdom past and present

"Perhaps your neighbor rolls in riches and you are poor. Your little house is close to a fine mansion and occasionally you look at that great estate where banquets are held. God has given your neighbor these gifts, so do not envy such wealth. Be content with what you have if you cannot better it. Do not wish for your neighbor to be like you are. Love him, and then you will not envy him."

Charles Haddon Spurgeon, *Morning and Evening*

truth tips

Cure for a Jealous Heart

▶ **STOP** feeling sorry for yourself because "the grass is greener in your neighbor's yard." Be satisfied with the gifts God has given you.

▶ **STOP** giving in to envy. Remember the Tenth Commandment and strive to be satisfied with the blessings God has bestowed on you.

▶ **STOP** comparing yourself to others and playing the performance game. Instead, be satisfied with the person God created you to be.

joy

"Rejoice always; pray without ceasing;
in everything give thanks; for this is
God's will for you in Christ Jesus."

—1 Thessalonians 5:16–18 NASB

"May the God of hope fill you with
all joy and peace as you trust in him,
so that you may overflow with hope
by the power of the Holy Spirit."

—Romans 15:13 NIV

"Then will I go unto the altar of God, unto
God my exceeding joy: yea, upon the harp
will I praise thee, O God my God."

—Psalm 43:4 KJV

wisdom past and present

"In this world everything is upside down. That
which, if it could be prolonged here, would be a
truancy, is likest that which in a better country is
the End of ends. Joy is the serious business of
Heaven."

C. S. Lewis, *Letters to Malcolm: Chiefly on Prayer*

truth tips

Choose the Joy of Christ

▶ **Study John 17:13 and Romans 8:16—17.** As a follower of Christ, you are a child of God and a joint heir of Jesus. You are no longer dead to your sin. Instead, you are made alive in Christ. This should produce in you pure joy!

▶ **Ask yourself three questions:** Am I experiencing divine joy—the kind that comes from a committed, unshakable relationship with Jesus? Am I too often satisfied with a joyless life? Do I know in my heart the joy of Christ—the kind that no circumstance in life can dispel?

loneliness

"I took you from the ends of the earth, from its farthest corners I called you. I said, 'You are my servant'; I have chosen you and have not rejected you. So do not fear, for I am with you; do not be dismayed, for I am your God."

—Isaiah 41:9–10 NIV

"I am with you always, even unto the end of the world."

—Matthew 28:20 KJV

wisdom past and present

"Avoiding both the risks of rejection and failure, some of us withdraw from virtually all meaningful interaction. We develop façades so that nobody can see our hurt. We may be socially active but not allow anyone to get really close to us. We are often afraid that if people really knew us, we would again experience hurt and rejection. Our deep sense of shame leads us to withdraw from others, we begin to feel isolated, and we experience the pain of loneliness."

Robert S. McGee, *The Search for Significance*

truth tips

Handling Loneliness: Questions to Consider

- What's making me feel so lonely? Am I home-sick? Am I anxious about something? Is some other unresolved issue at the root of my emotions?

- Am I not enough? Can't I find wholeness in the fact that I'm God's creation? Can't I still feel secure in my identity in Christ—even if that means being alone from time to time?

- What steps am I going to take to get through this loneliness?

- Do I feel lonely, anxious, or fearful more often than most people I know? Do I need professional help to work through these emotions?

lust

> "The mind of sinful man is death, but the mind controlled by the Spirit is life and peace."
>
> —Romans 8:6 NIV

> "For the grace of God that brings salvation has appeared to all men, teaching us that, denying ungodliness and worldly lusts, we should live soberly, righteously, and godly in the present age."
>
> —Titus 2:11–12 NKJV

reality bytes

Matt, 15, Kalamazoo, Michigan

For the longest time, I was convinced that God had made a big mistake with my life. Ever since I became a teenager, I often caught myself having thoughts about girls I know I shouldn't have. I couldn't stop thinking about sex, and I battled with lust everyday.

A lot of questions began to swirl through my mind: *Am I like other teens? Am I different? Am I normal sexually? Why does God let me suffer from such strong sexual urges? Why do I feel so guilty about my sexual appetite?*

Then my youth pastor gave me some comforting advice: "You're not alone, and God doesn't make mistakes. Most healthy, average teens have powerful desires for sex. It's nothing to be ashamed of. But it is a part of our lives that we MUST bring under God's control."

I took his advice and, with God's help, purity is now a priority in my life.

truth tips

Steps for Battling Lust

▸ Take a long, honest look at your sexuality. Then, accept the forgiveness of God and stop flogging yourself for your sexual failures. Persistent guilt and shame will make it difficult to shed sexual problems.

▸ Determine to change the way you think about the opposite sex. When you look at a guy or girl in sexual terms, "catch yourself" and train your mind to view others in non-sexual ways.

- Bring all your sexual thoughts and fantasies under conscious control by asking God to remind you when your thoughts need controlling.

- Acknowledge before God your lack of power to control your sexual urges, and pray that He will empower you to avoid temptation to sin by turning to healthy, wholesome activities.

- Keep in mind that sexual temptation is not sin. Some people are weakened by guilt from temptation. A pure mind is not a mind free of temptation. A pure mind chooses to act in the right way when temptation strikes.

- Steer clear of stuff that can feed your fantasies: movies, songs. . .steamy sites on the Internet.

- Watch what kind of friends you hang around with. Their language, habits, and humor will have an impact on you.

popularity

"Jesus said to them, 'Come with me. I'll make a new kind of fisherman out of you. I'll show you how to catch men and women instead of perch and bass.' They didn't ask questions, but simply dropped their nets and followed."

—Matthew 4:19–20 THE MESSAGE

"You are all sons of God through faith in Christ Jesus, for all of you who were baptized into Christ have clothed yourselves with Christ."

—Galatians 3:26–27 NIV

reality bytes

David, 14, Santa Rosa, California

Sometimes, I don't feel like I fit in. I look around school, and all I see are cliques and clones. The so-called "popular kids" (usually the jocks and prom queens) only hang out with other cool clones. The skaters, surfers, and metal heads are the misunderstood rebels. The science and computer kids just try to lie low somewhere in a corner. All they want to do is survive.

As for me—well, I feel as if I'm part of the middle mass of nothingness; someone who just blends into the tabletops. Sometimes I feel lost, lonely, and forgotten. At other times, I feel as if every eye is on ME—like I'm the featured act in today's teenage freak show!

Yet it's during those low points that I remind myself of an awesome truth: "This is how God showed his love among us: He sent his one and only Son into the world that we might live through him" (1 John 4:9 NIV). That's right! Jesus is crazy about weak, insecure, mixed-up me! So, why do I worry so much about what the crowd calls cool or popular?

truth tips

The Pain of Popularity

Beware: Too many people buy into the "popularity lie". . .

. . .the lie that they're worthless unless

they run with the popular crowd.

. . .the lie that cool equals having
a perfect body, possessing
Hollywood-caliber appeal, and
strutting past your peers with
a "party animal" reputation.

. . .the lie that measuring up as a person
means living up to an impossible,
even cruel, "cool code."

purity

> "Therefore, I urge you, brothers, in view of God's mercy, to offer your bodies as living sacrifices, holy and pleasing to God—this is your spiritual act of worship."
>
> —Romans 12:1 NIV

> "But immorality or any impurity or greed must not even be named among you, as is proper among saints."
>
> —Ephesians 5:3 NASB

reality bytes

Jaci, 17, Albuquerque, New Mexico

There are several reasons why purity is important to me. First, I believe that's the way God planned it. (It's sad that society has taken this beautiful gift and literally twisted it into something ugly.) Second, if we followed God's design for sex, there wouldn't be so many sexually transmitted diseases—and people wouldn't be dying of AIDS. Third, there wouldn't be as many unwanted pregnancies if single people honored purity. Bottom line: The safest sex is no sex until marriage. For me, I am definitely attracted to guys who are virgins. I feel that if I'm saving myself, he'd better be saving himself for me!

truth tips

Self-Control Is the Key

▶ **The apostle Paul gave us the prescription:** "It is God's will that you should be sanctified: that you should avoid sexual immorality; that each of you should learn to control his own body in a way that is holy and honorable, not in passionate lust like the heathen, who do not know God" (1 Thessalonians 4:3–5 NIV). Note: The operative words here are "each of you should learn to control his own body."

▶ **Make a pact for purity with your friends.** Acquire a cross necklace, a ring, or a watch beforehand, then vow to wear it as a symbol of your stand for purity. Read 2 Timothy 2:21–22 together and pray for each other.

vulnerability

> "Behold, I send you forth as sheep in
> the midst of wolves: be ye therefore wise
> as serpents, and harmless as doves."
>
> —Matthew 10:16 KJV

> "May our Lord Jesus Christ himself and
> God our Father, who loved us and by his
> grace gave us eternal encouragement and
> good hope, encourage your hearts and
> strengthen you in every good deed and
> word."
>
> —2 Thessalonians 2:16–17 NIV

wisdom past and present

"Although we are inclined to count our humanness
as vulnerability, in prayer it can be a source of
strength. The roles we play in life, however respon-
sibly, disguise the persons we are beneath our pos-
turings—cloaking us even from ourselves. God
formed us in our natures and characters, but God
did not create the roles we play in life. Even if our
scripts were thrust upon us by circumstances or by
others, we come to define and value ourselves by

our parts in life's drama—parent, breadwinner, patriot, householder, caretaker, lover, companion. . . . The quest for God through prayer is an adventure in stepping out of our assumed roles to communicate with God now and prepare for the time when we confront God face-to-face for eternity."

David Yount, *Breaking Through God's Silence*

truth tips

Be Victorious, Not Vulnerable

▸ **Clothe yourself in Christ.** You wouldn't leave your house without your pants or a shirt, right? Likewise, each morning when you get dressed, don't forget to put on Christ. (See Romans 13:14 for details.) Spend some time studying Scripture and praying. Wise Christians PRAY so they won't be up as PREY.

▸ **Walk with Christ.** When you're out in public, make sure others see Christ at work in your life—through your words and actions.

▸ **See yourself as Christ sees you.** Start by tuning in God's truth and tuning out the world's lies. Satan wants you to be weak, insecure, and vulnerable. Christ wants you to be strong, confident, and secure in Him.

chapter four

when it's hard

Facing Life's Challenges

addiction

"I do not understand what I do. For what
I want to do I do not do, but what I hate
I do. . . . For I have a desire to do what is
good, but I cannot carry it out. For what I
do is not the good I want to do; no, the
evil I do not want to do—this I keep on
doing. Now if I do what I do not want to
do, it is no longer I who do it but it is sin
living in me that does it."

—Romans 7:15, 18–20 NIV

"Because of the extravagance of those revela-
tions, and so I wouldn't get a big head, I was
given the gift of a handicap to keep me in
constant touch with my limitations. Satan's
angel did his best to get me down; what he
in fact did was push me to my knees. No
danger then of walking around high and
mighty! At first I didn't think of it as a gift,
and begged God to remove it. Three times I
did that, and then he told me,

'My grace is enough; it's all you need.
My strength comes into its own in your weakness.' "

—2 Corinthians 12:7–9 THE MESSAGE

"I am not being flippant when I say that all of us suffer from addiction. Nor am I reducing the meaning of addiction. I mean in all truth that the psychological, neurological, and spiritual dynamics of full-fledged addiction are actively at work in every human being. The same processes that are responsible for addiction to alcohol and narcotics are also responsible for addiction to ideas, work, relationships, power, moods, fantasies, and an endless variety of other things. We are all addicts in every sense of the word. Moreover, our addictions are our own worst enemies. They enslave us with chains that are of our own making and yet that, paradoxically, are virtually beyond our control. Addiction also makes idolators of us all, because it forces us to worship these objects of attachment, thereby preventing us from truly, freely loving God and one another. . . . Yet, in still another paradox, our addictions can lead us to a deep appreciation of grace. They can bring us to our knees."

Gerald G. May, M.D., *Addiction and Grace*

when it's hard

Five Healing Steps

- ▶ **Face the facts.** As Dr. May points out, all of us suffer from an addiction in one form or another: Perhaps it's a yearning for acceptance and approval or a desire to be popular. Some are addicted to their jobs or to a relationship, while others harbor secret addictions—pornography, lust, sex. And, of course, let's not forget the many addictions to substances—such as caffeine, sugar, nicotine, alcohol, drugs.

- ▶ **Evaluate yourself.** (1) Begin by asking yourself a few questions: *What kinds of addictions am I living with? Do others comment that I'm more attached to these things than I feel that I am? Am I afraid to confront the truth about these things? Am I willing to surrender all to Jesus Christ? Do I believe that Jesus is able to help me overcome anything that entangles my desires?* (2) Pull out a notepad and list your potential addictions, along with your thoughts, fears, and prayers regarding these matters.

- **Evaluate your faith.** Are your affections "nailed" to something or someone other than God? When push comes to shove, do you put your trust in the Holy Savior or do you retreat to other so-called "safe places"—the arms of a mate, the strength of your own abilities, comfort food? Are your addictions hindering your with walk with Christ?

- **Pray.** Pull off the masks, uncover the secrets, and pour out your heart to Jesus Christ. Don't hold back—confess everything. Ask Him to sever the chains that bind you. Ask Him for answers, strength, guidance, healing... true freedom. Then be willing to trust.

- **Seek counsel.** Whether it's a parent, a coach, a pastor, or a therapist, find a wise, trustworthy person who can help. Consider getting an accountability partner. (See page 194–195 for more on this topic.)

choices

> "For the LORD knoweth the way
> of the righteous: but the way of
> the ungodly shall perish."
>
> —Psalm 1:6 KJV

> " 'If anyone chooses to do God's will, he
> will find out whether my teaching comes
> from God or whether I speak on my own.
> He who speaks on his own does so to gain
> honor for himself, but he who works for the
> honor of the one who sent him is a man of
> truth; there is nothing false about him.' "
>
> —John 7:17–18 NIV

wisdom past and present

"A man is absent from church Sunday morning. Where is he? If he is in a hospital having his appendix removed, his absence tells us nothing about him except that he is ill; but if he is out on the golf course, that tells us a lot. To go to the hospital is compulsory; to go to the golf course, voluntary. The man is free to choose, and he chooses to play instead of to pray. His choice reveals what kind of man he is. Choices always do."

A. W. Tozer, *Tozer on Christian Leadership*

truth tips

Making Solid Choices

▶ **Live your own life**—don't just go along with the crowd. Get this: If you let someone push you into a choice when the pressure heats up, you'll have to deal with the consequences *all by yourself.*

▶ **Take responsibility for your actions.** What it all comes down to is this: You have to call the shots for yourself and take responsibility for what happens whether you like it or not.

▶ **Build a set of values right now.** Above all, think about your actions before you get into a tight spot. Weigh the consequences of your decisions before you act.

compromise

"What you're secretly thinking is
never going to happen. You're thinking:
'We're going to be like everybody else,
just like the other nations. We're going to
worship gods we can make and control.'
'As sure as I am the living God, says God,
the Master, think again!' "

—Ezekiel 20:32–33 THE MESSAGE

"No one can serve two masters. Either he
will hate the one and love the other, or he will
be devoted to the one and despise the other.
You cannot serve both God and Money."

—Matthew 6:24 NIV

wisdom past and present

"Your life has an influence on those around you. . . .
Your coworkers, your neighbors, and your friends
will all be impacted by your life. As the world tries
to persuade people to follow its standard, your life
should stand in stark contrast as an example of a
righteous person. Your life should convince those

around you of the wisdom of following God. Do not underestimate the positive effect that your obedience will have upon those close to you."

Henry T. Blackaby, *Experiencing God Day-By-Day*

truth tips

Five Ways to Know When It's a Compromise

- **Gut Instinct:** God gave you good sense. If it feels wrong, it probably is wrong.

- **Friend Factor:** Look at the advice you are getting and who it is coming from. Is it trustworthy? Are they looking out for your best interest—and for God's?

- **Prayer and Meditation:** Spend some time in prayer and quiet contemplation. Things have a way of revealing themselves when you're listening to God.

- **Word Search:** The Bible has an uncanny way of containing material relevant to your daily life.

- **Meet the Parents:** The shocking truth is—they actually know what they are talking about.

control

"These are all warning markers—
DANGER!—in our history books, written
down so that we don't repeat their mistakes.
Our positions in the story are parallel—
they at the beginning, we at the end—and
we are just as capable of messing it up as
they were. . . Forget about self-confidence;
it's useless. Cultivate God-confidence."

—1 Corinthians 10:11 THE MESSAGE

"The world and its desires pass
away, but the man who does
the will of God lives forever."

—1 John 2:17 NIV

reality bytes

Jamie, 16, Tacoma, Washington

As a senior, Jamie's chief goal this year is to
get accepted into a good art school. She
feels strongly that this is her key to a successful future, and she's willing to work as
hard as she can to make it happen. She

finds herself growing very frustrated when a project is returned to her marked with glaring red "B." Jamie's father tells her to keep trying her best, not to worry, and to let God control her future.

She shakes her head. "It's too hard," she says. "There has to be something I can do to make this happen."

truth tips

Who Has Control—You or God?

- Are you allowing Christ to complete God's will in your life?
- Are you resisting Christ—a path which would result in living outside the will of God?
- Are there promises God has made to you that you are refusing to allow Him to complete?
- Are there areas of your life that you need to release to Him?

courage

> " 'Be strong and of good courage, do not fear
> nor be afraid of them; for the LORD your
> God, He is the One who goes with you. He
> will not leave you nor forsake you.' "
>
> —Deuteronomy 31:6 NKJV

> " 'Fear not, for I have redeemed you;
> I have summoned you by name, you
> are mine. When you pass through the
> waters, I will be with you; and when
> you pass through the rivers, they will
> not sweep over you. When you walk
> through the fire, you will not be burned;
> the flames will not set you ablaze.' "
>
> —Isaiah 43:1–2 NIV

reality bytes

A Day in the Life of a Smoke Jumper

Dense, black, mushroom-shaped clouds rise
from a flaming landscape. Choppers and air
tankers tear through smoke-filled skies,
spraying bright red liquid on the inferno. A

short distance away, two twin-engine aircraft drop men, women, and supplies. One by one, thirty parachutists touch down on the scene—ready for combat.

In the war against wildfires, smoke jumpers are the air attack. Cuby Valdez is a member of an elite team of "forest paratroopers" stationed in Redmond, Oregon. The danger on the front lines can make even the toughest smoke jumper shake in his boots: Large fires generate one thousand-degree heat, hurricane-force winds, and thick, black plumes of smoke that choke away oxygen and sting the eyes.

As Cuby's feet hit the ground, his thoughts focus on a verse he had taped to one side of his helmet: "Be strong and courageous. Do not be terrified; do not be discouraged, for the LORD your God will be with you wherever you go" (Joshua 1:9 NIV).

truth tips

Choose Courage—Not Defeat

🔸 **Turn your problems over to God.** Are you experiencing pain? Problems? Pressures? Do you feel as if God has abandoned you? Choose courage—not defeat. You won't necessarily be freed from pain, but God will give you the grace to persevere.

▶ **Read Galatians 2:15—21.** As you study this passage, fix your eyes on Christ. Do you see Him hanging there on Calvary? Concentrate on His face until you see another face merge with His: your own. As a sinner, you have no choice but to die with Christ, then to live through Him.

▶ **Pray.** Ask Christ to give you courage—courage to face adversity, pain, fear. Then trust Him.

deception

"Indeed, all who desire to live godly in Christ Jesus will be persecuted. But evil men and impostors will proceed from bad to worse, deceiving and being deceived. You, however, continue in the things you have learned and become convinced of, knowing from whom you have learned them; and that from childhood you have known the sacred writings which are able to give you the wisdom that leads to salvation through faith which is in Christ Jesus."

—2 Timothy 3:12–15 NASB

"Therefore, laying aside all malice, all deceit, hypocrisy, envy, and all evil speaking, as newborn babes, desire the pure milk of the word, that you may grow thereby, if indeed you have tasted that the Lord is gracious."

—1 Peter 2:1–3 NKJV

wisdom past and present

"No one can deceive you unless he makes you think he is telling the truth. The unblushingly romantic has far less power to deceive than the apparently realistic."

C. S. Lewis, *An Experiment in Criticism*

truth tips

Two Ways to Avoid Being Deceived

▶ **Beware of Satan's tactics.** He knows just which buttons to push to tempt you away from depending on Christ. He has watched your behavior over the years and knows where you are weak. That's where he attacks.

▶ **Ask Christ for strength—especially for truth.** The Lord delivers His children from evil. But understand this: Merely hanging out at church and "doing your Christian duty" doesn't cut it. You need to know Jesus personally. He is the greatest conqueror ever, and with His guidance, you can have victory against the devil.

desire

> " Commit your works to the LORD and
> your plans will be established."
>
> —Proverbs 16:3 NASB

> "Forgetting what is behind and straining
> toward what is ahead, I press on toward
> the goal to win the prize for which God
> has called me heavenward in Christ Jesus."
>
> —Philippians 3:13–14 NIV

wisdom past and present

"We've been told that desire is the enemy. After all, desire is the single major hindrance to the goal— getting us in line. And so, we are told to kill desire and call it sanctification. But God is not the enemy of desire. 'Delight yourself also in the LORD,' the psalmist tells us, 'and He shall give you the desires of your heart' (Psalm 37:4 NKJV). God is the One who made these deep hearts within us, created us as men and women with these deep longings. And though we turned our backs on Him, He pursued us, called us back to His own good heart and intends to bring us life again. This is why holiness is not deadness; it is passion. It is being *more* attuned to our desires, to what we were truly made for and therefore what we really want."

John Eldredge, *Dare to Desire*

truth tips

Seven Realities About Dreams and Desires

- No dream is too big for God.

- Our Heavenly Father wants to be the author of *all* your desires.

- The Lord's desires for your life are better than your greatest goals.

- Successful Christians ask, "Lord, what plans do You have for my life?"—not "How can I fit You into my plans?"

- Once you've considered your gifts and talents, commit them to God. (He will direct your steps.)

- God will open and close the right doors of opportunity as you launch out in faith.

- If you ask, the Lord will reveal what His good, pleasing, and perfect will looks like for you (Romans 12:2).

doubt

"But let him ask in faith without doubting. For the doubter is like the surging sea, driven and tossed by the wind. That person should not expect to receive anything from the Lord. An indecisive man is unstable in all his ways."

—James 1:6–8 HCSB

"If we take human testimony at face value, how much more should we be reassured when God gives testimony as he does here, testifying concerning his Son. Whoever believes in the Son of God inwardly confirms God's testimony. Whoever refuses to believe in effect calls God a liar, refusing to believe God's own testimony regarding his Son."

—1 John 5:9–10 THE MESSAGE

reality bytes

Amber, 14, St. Louis, Missouri

Amber slammed the Bible shut and flopped on her bed. "Get real!" she grumbled. "I could NEVER be like that dusty old Bible guy!"

She rested her chin on her knee and prayed. "God, I'm NOT Jeremiah, and I don't think I'll ever measure up. That guy lived thousands of years ago. This is the twenty-first century. Jeremiah didn't have to put up with all the jerks at Marshall Junior High. And Jeremiah didn't have to take summer school to pass English."

She cracked open her Bible once more and reread the part that bugged her: "But the LORD said to me, 'Do not say, "I am only a child." You must go to everyone I send you to and say whatever I command you. Do not be afraid of them, for I am with you and will rescue you,' declares the LORD" (Jeremiah 1:7 NIV).

Amber clicked off her lamp and slid under the covers. The moment her head hit the pillow, dozens of scenes from the day started flipping through her mind. She saw Kathy and Gina rolling their eyes at her for not cheating and cutting class with them. And Gina's words rang over and over in her ears, "Loosen up, Amber. You're such a goody-goody church girl."

Amber prayed once more. "Lord, this

Christian thing is too hard. I can't do it by myself. Please help. Please take away the doubts."

With that, Amber squeezed shut her eyes and drifted off to sleep.

truth tips

Dealing with Doubts

▶ **Follow Amber's example and pray.** Do you have doubts about the Lord's power in your life? Are you a chameleon for Christ—a member of God's secret service? Understand that the Lord hasn't abandoned you. He cares about you more than you can ever imagine.

▶ **Know that feelings do not equal faith.** Your faith is based on the unchangeable truth that God came to earth in Jesus, died for your sins, rose again from the dead, and even today reigns as Lord over all. Nothing can change this truth. Not feelings, not indigestion, not bad hair days, not lousy school days.

▶ **If your faith is stuck in dreamland, it's**

time to wake up. Accepting Christ in your heart is the best thing you've ever done. Don't worry so much about being ridiculed and rejected when you don't go along with the crowd. Jesus won't leave you all alone. You've got to trust God and take some risks.

failure

"Trust in the LORD with all your heart and
lean not on your own understanding;
in all your ways acknowledge him,
and he will make your paths straight."

—Proverbs 3:5–6 NIV

"Cast all your anxiety on him because
he cares for you."

—1 Peter 5:7 NIV

wisdom past and present

"Failure, like fumbles, is part of the game. What
matters is how you go about recovering possession. Read Proverbs 3:5-6, my life verse, for more
clues on handling failure. Above all, get on with
your life instead of trying to relive what is gone
for good."

Mike Holmgren, NFL coach,
"Breakaway's Guide to an Amazing Life," *Breakaway* magazine

truth tips

Five Ways to Handle Failure

▶ Don't just internalize or ignore your mistakes. Face them, and admit that you're disappointed—even angry—with your circumstances.

▶ Share your pain with someone you trust.

▶ Determine to learn what you can from failure. Losing hurts more than winning feels good, but the hurt is often what God uses to get your attention.

▶ Focus on your strengths.

▶ Expect failure to knock on your door again. It knows where you live.

future

"Watch the blameless and observe
the upright, for the man of peace
will have a future."

—Psalm 37:37 HCSB

"Surely there is a future, and your hope
will not be cut off."

—Proverbs 23:18 NASB

wisdom past and present

"It will take us a couple of decades to get out of
the swamp of what's called *postmodernism*—a
recently developed post-Christian philosophy in
which relativism is all and you have no notion of
absolute truth. In the churches, we will have to be
constantly speaking against that because God
does speak truth, and the Christian faith is thus
what Francis Schaeffer called 'the truth,' that is,
permanent, transcultural, transhistorical *truth*—
truth that abides."

J. I. Packer, *J. I. Packer Answers Questions for Today*

truth tips

Future Quest: A Road Map to Success

▶ **Ask yourself this question:** "Is the Lord directing my steps?" If so, Proverbs 16:3 (NIV) promises that you're on the right track: "Commit to the LORD whatever you do, and your plans will succeed." But keep in mind that your plans have no strength if they're not from God.

▶ **Pursue what is kind, just, and loving in life:** "Better a little with righteousness than much gain with injustice" (Proverbs 16:8 NIV).

▶ **Be still and listen.** Get away regularly and have a personal retreat. Find a quiet place where you can focus on His voice and direction for your life.

▶ **Map out what you sense God is telling you.** Putting down your future plans on paper will help you to clarify and understand them. It can also help you to remember your goals even when circumstances look discouraging.

identity

"For you created my inmost being; you knit me together in my mother's womb. I praise you because I am fearfully and wonderfully made; your works are wonderful, I know that full well. My frame was not hidden from you when I was made in the secret place. When I was woven together in the depths of the earth, your eyes saw my unformed body. All the days ordained for me were written in your book before one of them came to be."

—Psalm 139:13–16 NIV

wisdom past and present

"We were all created to be God's image-bearers. That means that we were created to seek and find God through seeking and finding the truth about God. We are made in such a way, I believe, that we are only at peace with ourselves when it's God's truth that our minds are grasping and consciously obeying. Human life is lacking dignity until you get to that point."

J. I. Packer, *J. I. Packer Answers Questions for Today*

truth tips

How to Refocus Your Identity

▶ **Be YOU, but be REAL.** It's okay to express
yourself through the clothes you wear or to
excel at a sport or a hobby. But if you try to
base your total identity on those things,
you'll end up losing your identity—not to
mention being bitterly disappointed.

▶ **Find yourself in Christ.** The Lord doesn't
look at you and say, "This is who you are—
and who you'll always be." Instead, He says,
"Just imagine who you can become!"

▶ **Know the secret to success.** Grounding your
identity in God is the key to handling any
struggle. (For a clue, see 1 John 3:1.)

▶ **Know the truth.** You are valuable to God—
regardless of how you look, how smart you
are, what you do, and whether your life is full
of successes or failures.

materialism

" 'Take heed and beware of covetousness,
for one's life does not consist in the
abundance of the things he possesses.' "

—Luke 12:15 NKJV

"For the love of money is the root of all evil:
which while some coveted after, they have
erred from the faith, and pierced themselves
through with many sorrows."

—1 Timothy 6:10 KJV

wisdom past and present

"Though most of us do not live as nomads, we
still need to ask, *Is my faith being buried by my possessions? Is my faith shattered most when my finan-
cial situation looks the bleakest? Do I define my
security by what I have stored in the bank?* By themselves, possessions aren't sinful, but our faith is
buried when we begin to worship things."

Franklin Graham, *Living Beyond the Limits*

truth tips

Finding Balance in a Material World

▶ **Don't buy the worldly lies.** Beauty, brains, bucks. Why do so many people in this world place such high value on these three attributes? Keep in mind that, in the crowd's eyes, your value is wrapped up in what you do, how smart or athletic you are, and how you look.

▶ **Focus on the truth.** In God's eyes, what matters is who you are—His child. Read Romans 12:9–16. Based on this passage, what qualities are most important to God?

▶ **Let God be God.** Ask Him to tear down idols in your life—a relationship, a job, a possession... anything that you value more than Him.

pain

"Surely He has borne our griefs and carried our sorrows; yet we esteemed Him stricken, smitten by God, and afflicted. But He was wounded for our transgressions, He was bruised for our iniquities; the chastisement for our peace was upon Him, and by His stripes we are healed."

—Isaiah 53:4–5 NKJV

"Dear friends, do not be surprised at the painful trial you are suffering, as though something strange were happening to you. But rejoice that you participate in the sufferings of Christ, so that you may be overjoyed when his glory is revealed."

—1 Peter 4:12–13 NIV

wisdom past and present

"I've met so many innocent sufferers who seem to be gladly offering their pain to God in Christ as part of the Atonement, so patient, so meek, even so at peace, and so unselfish that we can hardly doubt they are being, as St. Paul says, 'made perfect by suffering.' On the other hand, I meet selfish egoists in whom suffering seems to produce only resentment, hate, blasphemy, and more egoism. They are the real problem."

C. S. Lewis, *Letters of C. S. Lewis*

truth tips

The Problem with Pain—and the Solution!

▶ **Jesus shares your pain.** He puts Himself in your shoes and feels everything that you feel.

▶ **Christ is the Father of "suffering with"—** and the God of all comfort!

▶ **God molds your character.** When the Lord comes beside you and offers the strength to take your next step, you learn to walk with fellow sufferers—to let their pain become your pain.

perseverance

"For you have need of endurance, so that
when you have done the will of God, you
may receive what was promised."

—Hebrews 10:36 NASB

"Therefore we do not lose heart. Though
outwardly we are wasting away, yet inwardly
we are being renewed day by day. For our
light and momentary troubles are achieving
for us an eternal glory that far outweighs
them all. So we fix our eyes not on what is
seen, but on what is unseen. For what is seen
is temporary, but what is unseen is eternal."

—2 Corinthians 4:16–18 NIV

wisdom past and present

"I have climbed my mountains and have seen the
other side. I have dodged thunderstorms, battled
blizzards, endured incredible pain, and faced my
fears through faith in God. Through it all, I have
gained a deeper experience with God. Time after
time, when it seemed the expedition was doomed,

He smoothed the way. Time after time, when my body hurt so badly that I thought I couldn't take another step, He infused me with the strength to continue. Time after time, He was there."

Todd Huston, "More Than Mountains," *Breakaway* magazine

truth tips

Two Thoughts About Pressing On

- **The Way of Christ is the narrow way.** (See Matthew 7:13–14 and John 15:18–21.) Jesus promised His disciples pain and suffering, not a life of comfort.

- **Christ will give you the strength to press on.** (See 1 Peter 5:4.) Christ gives joy and victory to those who persevere. The narrow way leads to eternal life.

pressure

"And do not be drunk with wine, in which
is dissipation; but be filled with the Spirit,
speaking to one another in psalms and
hymns and spiritual songs, singing and making melody in your heart to the Lord, giving
thanks always for all things to God the Father
in the name of our Lord Jesus Christ."

—Ephesians 5:18–20 NKJV

"For the grace of God that brings salvation
has appeared to all men. It teaches us to say
'No' to ungodliness and worldly passions,
and to live self-controlled, upright and
godly lives in this present age, while we
wait for the blessed hope—the glorious
appearing of our great God and Savior,
Jesus Christ, who gave himself for us to
redeem us from wickedness and to purify
for himself a people that are his very own,
eager to do what is good."

—Titus 2:11–14 NIV

reality bytes

Jeff, 18, Tampa Bay, Florida

Sun. Sand. Surf. A dreamy stretch of Florida beach is exactly what Jeff had in mind for this year's spring break bash. So why is he sitting in the back of a police car—instead of riding the waves?

"The guys and I got caught drinking in public," the embarrassed eighteen-year-old tells his parents later. "The crazy thing is, we're all Christians. I should have said no when they handed me the first beer. I guess I got caught up in the moment and just wasn't thinking straight."

truth tips

How to Unplug Peer Pressure

◗ Build a set of values right now.

◗ Think about your actions *before* you get in a tight spot.

◗ Weigh the consequences of your decisions before you act and find the hidden dangers before they sneak up on you.

◗ Know the truth: By preplanning your response and having your values thought out beforehand, you are more prepared to act as you want to act—not as the group wants you to act.

rejection

"For the sake of his great name the LORD
will not reject his people, because the
LORD was pleased to make you his own."

—1 Samuel 12:22 NIV

"I will not leave you comfortless:
I will come to you."

—John 14:18 KJV

reality bytes

Jason, 16, Kansas City, Missouri

Jason can't sleep. His mind is racing full
speed with haunting scenes from the day.
Ever since committing his life to Jesus at a
youth retreat, Jason has been catching heat
from the other guys on the football team.

"Man, you're insane!"

"Jason's gone religious on us."

"We thought you were a jock, not a
'Jesus Freak.'"

Jason stares at the Bible on his bedside
table. It looks so weird sitting there. He

thinks of the youth meeting coming up next week (and his pledge to say a few words).

What have I done? he wonders. *And what am I gonna do?*

truth tips

Handling Rejection: Two Questions to Ask

▶ **"Is my focus on the world?"** Do you care more about the opinions of others—to the point of putting them before God? Or are you willing to give all to Christ—to begin trusting Him? Consider these words from a fellow saint: "He is no fool who gives up what he cannot keep. . .to gain what he cannot lose."

▶ **"Am I treating my relationship with God like a passing fad?"** Know this: Your faith in Christ is a step-by-step, day-by-day *commitment*. And like any relationship, it requires your time and devotion in order for it to grow. "Test everything. Hold on to the good. Avoid every kind of evil" (1 Thessalonians 5:21–22 NIV). You may even be rejected for your faith.

silence

> " 'But the LORD is in his holy temple;
> let all the earth be silent before him.' "
>
> —Habakkuk 2:20 NIV

"Be still, and know that I am God:
I will be exalted among the heathen,
I will be exalted in the earth."

—Psalm 46:10 KJV

wisdom past and present

"Monastic life, as presented by Saint Benedict, offered a situation wherein the needs of the heart, the mind, and the physical body would all be met. *'Cruce, libro, et atro,'* 'Cross, book, and plow,' was the motto. Ample time was devoted each day to prayer, study, and physical work. Most activities not involving the proclamation of Scripture were carried out without speaking, and each day the Great Silence was observed from the end of Compline until the end of Lauds. These periods of quiet, which were strictly enforced, provided space for each individual to look within, both for forgiveness of sins and for the deepening assurance of God's imminent presence. They also helped the monks 'to utter truth from the heart and mouth' when they did speak."

Katharine Le Mee, Chant

truth tips

Hearing God Through the Silence

▶ **Let God tear down the "giant invisible wall" that separates you from Him.** How? Go to Christ in prayer. Unload the guilt and shame in your life.

▶ **Confess everything.** Tell Him all about your sins, tell Him you're sorry, and He'll forgive you. In Jesus, you'll find acceptance, love, and freedom—despite your shortcomings.

▶ **Be still and listen.** Once you've opened up your heart to God, sit back and be silent. Allow Him to speak to you. Tune in His voice, and listen to His direction.

temptation

"No temptation has seized you except what is common to man. And God is faithful; he will not let you be tempted beyond what you can bear. But when you are tempted, he will also provide a way out so that you can stand up under it."

—1 Corinthians 10:13 NIV

"For in that He Himself has suffered, being tempted, He is able to aid those who are tempted."

—Hebrews 2:18 NKJV

reality bytes

Tanya, 16, Los Angeles, California

Tanya is tempted to do it. What she desperately needs is sitting on the desk in front of her: the answers to tomorrow's American Literature exam. Mrs. Rogers, her teacher, has stepped out of the room for about ten minutes. Tanya is alone.

Her teacher invited her to stop by

her class after school to work on an extra-credit essay. With an F in American Literature, Tanya needs all the help she can get. But this is way too easy!

It could solve my problems, she tells herself, keeping an eye on the door. *But it would be cheating. Yet I did pray this morning, asking God to help me pass this class.*

Deep inside, Tanya knows cheating is wrong and that God would have no part in it. Still, the thought of being held back stabs at her insides. *I could jot down a few answers—enough to help me pass.*

Just as Tanya puts her hand on the answer sheet, the door opens.

"I'm back! So how's it going—?" Mrs. Rogers stops in mid-sentence and gasps.

Tanya swallows hard and squeezes her eyes shut. *Oh, man—what have I done?*

truth tips

Toppling Temptation: Two Keys

▸ **Make a pact.** Get your Christian friends together. Discuss things you've all struggled with as a result of peer pressure. Sign an agreement to hold each other accountable in these areas. Knowing others agree with you will help you stand firm when pressure sets in.

▶ **Ask God for help.** In your quiet times, ask God to remind you of your standards. Ask Him to strengthen you as He did the early disciples when they were faced with pressure to stop preaching the gospel.

warfare

"He who dwells in the shelter of the Most
High will rest in the shadow of the
Almighty. I will say of the LORD, 'He is my
refuge and my fortress, my God, in whom
I trust.' Surely he will save you from the
fowler's snare and from the deadly pestilence.
He will cover you with his feathers, and
under his wings you will find refuge; his
faithfulness will be your shield and rampart."

—Psalm 91:1–4 NIV

" 'Fear nothing in the things you're about to
suffer—but stay on guard! Fear nothing! The
Devil is about to throw you in jail for a time
of testing. . . . Don't quit, even if it costs you
your life. Stay there believing. I have a Life-
Crown sized and ready for you.' "

—Revelation 2:10 THE MESSAGE

wisdom past and present

"When the light comes, the darkness must depart.
Where truth is, the lie must flee. If the lie

remains, there will be a severe conflict, because truth cannot and will not lower its standard. If you follow Christ, all the hounds of the world will yelp at your heels."

Charles H. Spurgeon, *Morning and Evening*

truth tips

Winning the War

When we trust God completely, He works things out perfectly. It's easy to allow ourselves to be overly concerned about the unknown—especially spiritual warfare. But it's really not our problem. It's God's. He will take care of you. The Lord has armed every Christian with spiritual weapons packed with "divine power":

- **The sword of the spirit— the Holy Bible.**

- **Prayer.** Colossians 3:16 (NASB) tells Christians to "let the word of Christ richly dwell within you."

- **Supernatural peace.** Philippians 4:7 (NIV) promises that "the peace of God. . .will guard your hearts and your minds in Christ Jesus."

chapter five

why they matter

matter

Making Eternal Connections

accountability

"Therefore, since we are surrounded by such a great cloud of witnesses, let us throw off everything that hinders and the sin that so easily entangles, and let us run with perseverance the race marked out for us. Let us fix our eyes on Jesus, the author and perfecter of our faith, who for the joy set before him endured the cross, scorning its shame, and sat down at the right hand of the throne of God. Consider him who endured such opposition from sinful men, so that you will not grow weary and lose heart."

—Hebrews 12:1–3 NIV

"And He said to me, 'It is done! I am the Alpha and the Omega, the Beginning and the End. I will give to the thirsty from the spring of living water as a gift. The victor will inherit these things, and I will be his God, and he will be My son. But the cowards, unbelievers, vile, murderers, sexually immoral, sorcerers, idolaters, and all liars— their share will be in the lake that burns with fire and sulfur, which is the second death.' "

—Revelation 21:6–8 HCSB

"A true friend is one who hears and understands when you share your deepest feelings. He supports you when you are struggling; he corrects you, gently and with love, when you err; and he forgives you when you fail. A true friend prods you to personal growth, stretches you to your full potential. And most amazing of all, he celebrates your successes as if they were his own."

Richard Exley, *Your Bridge to a Better Future*

truth tips

How to Build Accountability

▶ **Seek out a true friend**—a solid, mature Christian who will help you build strength through Christ.

▶ **Set a time to meet regularly.** When the two of you get together, be willing to talk about anything.

▶ **Pray daily for each other.**

why they matter

authorities

"But Peter and the apostles replied, 'We must obey God rather than men. The God of our fathers raised up Jesus, whom you had murdered by hanging Him on a tree. God exalted this man to His right hand as ruler and Savior, to grant repentance to Israel, and forgiveness of sins. We are witnesses of these things, and so is the Holy Spirit whom God has given to those who obey Him.' "

—Acts 5:29–32 HCSB

"Servants, do what you're told by your earthly masters. And don't just do the minimum that will get you by. Do your best. Work from the heart for your real Master, for God, confident that you'll get paid in full when you come into your inheritance. Keep in mind always that the ultimate Master you're serving is Christ."

—Colossians 3:22–24 THE MESSAGE

wisdom past and present

"Faith points to a moral law beyond man's law and calls us to duties higher than material gain. Freedom of religion is not something to be feared; it's to be welcomed, because faith gives us a moral core and teaches us to hold ourselves to high standards, to love and to serve others, and to live responsible lives. . . ."

President George W. Bush, quoted from a speech at China's Tsinghua University, February 22, 2002

truth tips

"Whom Should I Follow?"
(Three Questions to Ask)

- Is this particular authority in my life (parent, teacher, employer) asking me to do something immoral, something that would cause me to sin and to disobey God?

- Will I glorify God by obeying this "earthly master"?

- What would Jesus do?

" 'Father, I want those you have given me to
be with me where I am, and to see my glory,
   the glory you have given me because you
loved me before the creation of the world.' "

—John 17:24 NIV

"Hitherto have ye asked nothing in
my name: ask, and ye shall receive,
that your joy may be full."

—John 16:24 KJV

reality bytes

Rich, 18, Sandwich, Massachusetts

*Ewing's Sarcoma—bone cancer?! At my
age?* The news from Rich's doctor was
almost too hard to believe. But after sur-
gery (to remove a tumor) and months of
chemo treatments, Rich beat the odds.
God spared his life.

   One evening, while sitting alone in his
hospital room, Rich bowed his head and

began to pour out his heart to God. "First of all, I want to thank You for letting me live," he began. "I didn't know if I'd wake up again, but when I opened my eyes, I saw my family staring back at me. Thank You so much for that." Tears formed in the corner of Rich's eyes as he paused and lifted the sheet covering his legs. "I hate to ask for more, but I still really need Your help, Lord," Rich whispered. "As You know, the doctors say I won't be able to ever run, jump, or bike again. They say I'll need to use a cane for the rest of my life just to hobble around. But I don't want to hobble. I'm 18! My friends are having fun, meeting people, taking classes, living life! I want to live life, too—a normal life. Please help me, God," Rich pleaded. "Please give me the strength to recuperate and the patience to know I can't improve overnight. Amen." In the weeks that followed, God answered his prayer—walking him through the pain, step by step.

"Defeating a Killer," *Breakaway* magazine

brokenhearted

"Yea, though I walk through the valley
of the shadow of death, I will fear
no evil: for thou art with me; thy rod
and thy staff they comfort me."

—Psalm 23:4 KJV

"He heals the brokenhearted
and binds up their wounds."

—Psalm 147:3 NIV

wisdom past and present

"Christ is not a magic wand that can be waved over our heartaches and headaches to make them disappear. 'In [Him] are hidden all the treasures of wisdom and knowledge' (Colossians 2:3 NIV). Wisdom and knowledge, including knowing how to be content, are hidden in Him, like a treasure that needs to be searched for. . . . As we wrap our hands around the task and, in faith, begin to exert force, eureka! Divine energy surges through us. God's strength works in us at the moment we exercise faith for the task."

Joni Eareckson Tada, *When God Weeps*

truth tips

Five Truths for the Brokenhearted

- God is close to the brokenhearted.
- God struggles with us as we struggle.
- God uses pain in our lives to strengthen us.
- God gives us the strength to endure any problem.
- God is our healer.

christlikeness

"You also became imitators of us and of the Lord, having received the word in much tribulation with the joy of the Holy Spirit, so that you became an example to all the believers in Macedonia and in Achaia."

—1 Thessalonians 1:6–7 NASB

"But also for this very reason, giving all diligence, add to your faith virtue, to virtue knowledge, to knowledge self-control, to self-control perseverance, to perseverance godliness, to godliness brotherly kindness, and to brotherly kindness love. For if these things are yours and abound, you will be neither barren nor unfruitful in the knowledge of our Lord Jesus Christ."

—2 Peter 1:5–8 NKJV

reality bytes

Craig, 18, Quezon City, Philippines

"Growing up immersed in the culture of a

third-world country opened my eyes to the endless need for a Savior in the hearts of these people. As I watched my parents and their passion for missions, I often wondered if God could use me in the Philippines. Every day as I commute to school, street children press their faces against our van window and tap lightly on the glass begging for money. It can become an ignored routine of everyday annoyance—or those soft taps on our window can echo in my head and plague me with a longing to help these poverty-stricken people."

truth tips

Keys to Being Christlike

▶ **Strive to be an encourager.** Now more than ever the world needs encouragers—Christlike people who offer kindness and compassion, authentic Christians who are willing to reach out to those who have been wounded by discouragers. Ask the Lord to show you how to be merciful, just as He is merciful. Consider this: He reaches out to the unlovable, befriends those the world

would rather forget, and touches those who
seem untouchable.

- **Set the example for others.** Living a double
life is a surefire way to blow your witness—
especially to a non-Christian. Remember,
others are watching you.

church

> "See to it that no one takes you captive through hollow and deceptive philosophy, which depends on human tradition and the basic principles of this world rather than on Christ."
>
> —Colossians 2:8 NIV

> "And He Himself gave some to be apostles, some prophets, some evangelists, and some pastors and teachers, for the equipping of the saints for the work of ministry, for the edifying of the body of Christ, till we all come to the unity of the faith and of the knowledge of the Son of God, to a perfect man, to the measure of the stature of the fullness of Christ."
>
> —Ephesians 4:11–13 NKJV

wisdom past and present

"For all our churches to grow, we must constantly pray for the people in our city; plan and implement our strategies; and utilize every opportunity to get the gospel into our community at large."

Ted Haggard, *Loving Your City Into the Kingdom*

truth tips

Why Plugging Into Church Is Important

- **Worshipping God is an interactive experience.** It's meant to be shared with others. Get this: Heaven is going to be packed with all kinds of people praising and worshipping God.

- **Our church family keeps us accountable.** We encounter a lot of distractions during the week—in a classroom, at work, on TV, with our friends. Gathering with a church body plugs us back into God's truth.

- **Church gives us a chance to be fed from God's Word.** Getting a solid spiritual diet nourishes our souls.

i believe

community

"The body is a unit, though it is made up of
many parts; and though all its parts are
many, they form one body. So it is with
Christ. Now you are the body of Christ,
and each one of you is a part of it."

—1 Corinthians 12:12, 27 NIV

"So then, while we have opportunity, let us
do good to all people, and especially to those
who are of the household of the faith."

—Galatians 6:10 NASB

wisdom past and present

"I can do what you can't do, and you can do what
I can't do. *Together* we can do great things."

Mother Teresa, *Your Bridge to a Better Future*

truth tips

Ten Ways to Be a Light in Your Community

▶ Get to know someone you normally wouldn't
   hang out with: the loner in the back of the
   class, the kid everyone picks on.

▶ Pray with a hurting neighbor.

▶ Volunteer to shovel snow from a stranger's
   driveway.

▶ Visit a shut-in.

▶ Send your parents on a date—and pay for it!

▶ Help out at a church function.

▶ Make food for someone.

▶ Buy a meal for a homeless person.

▶ Help a friend clean his room or do homework.

▶ Do something extraordinary, something
   someone might never expect.

discipleship

"He makes my feet like the feet of a deer
and sets me securely on the heights. He
trains my hands for war; my arms can bend
a bow of bronze. You have given me the
shield of Your salvation; Your right hand
upholds me, and Your humility exalts me.
You widen [a place] beneath me for my
steps, and my ankles do not give way.

—Psalm 18:33–36 HCSB

"With what shall I come before the LORD,
and bow myself before the High God? Shall
I come before Him with burnt offerings,
with calves a year old? Will the LORD be
pleased with thousands of rams, ten thou-
sand rivers of oil? Shall I give my firstborn
for my transgression, the fruit of my body
for the sin of my soul? He has shown you, O
man, what is good; and what does the LORD
require of you but to do justly, to love mercy,
and to walk humbly with your God?"

—Micah 6:6–8 NKJV

wisdom past and present

"Discipleship is more than acquiring head knowledge and memorizing Scripture verses. It is learning to give Jesus Christ total access to your life so He will live His life through you. Your greatest difficulty will be believing that your relationship with Christ is at the heart of your Christian life. When others watch you face a crisis, do they see the risen Lord responding? Does your family see the difference Christ makes when you face a need? What difference does the presence of Jesus Christ make in your life? God wants to reveal Himself to those around you working mightily through you."

Henry T. Blackaby, *Experiencing God Day-By-Day*

truth tips

Three Keys to Effective Discipleship

🔹 **Be faithful.** Deepening your walk with God happens when you trust that He is in your life, even when you don't sense His presence; even when He seems a million miles away.

🔹 **Be available.** Make knowing Him *the priority* in your life 24/7. Be available daily by spending time reading the Bible, praying, and worshipping Him.

▶ **Be teachable.** Before you begin studying Scripture, pray something like this: "Lord, help me to concentrate today. I want to tune into Your voice and Your instruction for my life. Draw me close to You and transform me into the kind of person You want me to be. Amen."

family

"God sets the lonely in families. . .but the
rebellious live in a sun-scorched land."

—Psalm 68:6 NIV

"A wise son accepts his father's discipline,
but a scoffer does not listen to rebuke."

—Proverbs 13:1 NASB

wisdom past and present

"It's easy to think that the world revolves around
you. That everything on the earth, including your
family, was put here so your needs could be met. But
peaceful families are families where the individual
members are thinking about the needs of others—
not themselves. Plus, a cooperative attitude may
increase the chances of your parents giving you more
privileges in the future. . . . It's important to know
that your relationship with your brothers and sisters
will have a direct effect on your relationship with
your mother and father. Few things can cause a parent to become a raving maniac quicker than constant bickering and fighting. If you learn to fight

with your brothers and sisters less frequently, you'll notice a change in your parents. The glassy gaze and the dark circles beneath their eyes will disappear. Their voices will become much quieter, and they won't foam at the mouth as often."

Ken Davis, *How to Live with Your Parents*
without Losing Your Mind

truth tips

A Three-Point Strategy for
Handling Home Front Hassles

▶ Commit your life to the Lord, turn away from sin, and seek God for answers.

▶ Understand that no problem is too big for God to handle—not even a fight with Mom or Dad. God will set you on the right course if you let Him.

▶ Seek unity and solutions to problems, not strife and pointless quarrels.

friends

"As iron sharpens iron,
so one man sharpens another."

—Proverbs 27:17 NIV

"Two are better than one, because they have
a good return for their work: If one falls
down, his friend can help him up."

—Ecclesiastes 4:9–10 NIV

wisdom past and present

"According to Scripture, a friend is one who challenges you to become all that God intends. Jonathan could have succeeded his father to become the next king of Israel. But he loved his friend David, and he encouraged him to follow God's will, even though it meant Jonathan would forfeit his own claim to the throne (1 Samuel 19:1–7). The mark of biblical friends is that their friendship draws you closer to Christ. They 'sharpen' you and motivate you to do what is right. True friends tell you the truth and even risk hurting your feelings because they love you and have your best interests at heart (Proverbs 27:6)."

Henry T. Blackaby, *Experiencing God Day-By-Day*

truth tips

Sorting Out Friends from Phonies

▶ **Take inventory of your friendships.** Is popularity more important than genuine friendship? If your friends are leading you in the wrong direction and you continue to follow, beware: You're not living your life anymore—the crowd is. (And when it comes time to pay the price for your actions, you end up doing it all by yourself.)

▶ **Sever bad ties— before you get tied up.** When God says one thing in the Bible and your friends say another, then you must follow God and let your friends leave you if they wish. It's a hard choice, but one Christians sometimes have to make.

▶ **Seek Christian friends who share your values.** And spend less time with friends who aren't interested in pursuing a godly walk. Like it or not, the people you spend time with have a big influence on your life.

heroes

"Be imitators of God, therefore, as dearly
loved children and live a life of love, just as
Christ loved us and gave himself up for us as
a fragrant offering and sacrifice to God."

—Ephesians 5:1–2 NIV

"These all died in faith, not having received
the promises, but having seen them afar off
were assured of them, embraced them and
confessed that they were strangers and pil-
grims on the earth. For those who say such
things declare plainly that they seek a home-
land. And truly if they had called to mind
that country from which they had come
out, they would have had opportunity to
return. But now they desire a better, that is,
a heavenly country. Therefore God is not
ashamed to be called their God, for He has
prepared a city for them."

—Hebrews 11:13–16 NKJV

wisdom past and present

"Our generation has never seen a man crucified except in sugary religious art. . . . A crucified slave beside the Roman road screamed until his voice died and then hung, a filthy, festering clot of flies, sometimes for days—a living man whose hands and feet were swollen masses of gangrenous meat. That is what our Lord took upon Himself, 'that through death he might destroy him that had the power of death, that is, the devil; and deliver them, who through fear of death were all their lifetime subject to bondage.' 'Thou shalt not' is the beginning of wisdom. But the end of wisdom, the new law, is 'Thou shalt.' To be Christian is to be old? Not a bit of it. To be Christian is to be reborn, and free, and unafraid, and immortally young" (Hebrews 2:14–15 KJV).

Joy Davidman, *Smoke on the Mountain*

truth tips

How to Be a Hero

▶ **Have compassion for others.** Ask the Lord to show you how to be merciful, just as He is merciful.

▶ **Reach out!** Consider this: God reaches out to the unlovable, befriends those the world would rather forget, and touches those who seem untouchable.

▶ **Set the standard.** Living a double life is a surefire way to blow your witness—especially to a non-Christian. Remember, others are watching you.

integrity

"The man of integrity walks securely, but he who takes crooked paths will be found out."

—Proverbs 10:9 NIV

"Behold, God will not cast away the blameless, nor will He uphold the evildoers."

—Job 8:20 NKJV

"Do everything without complaining or arguing, so that you may become blameless and pure, children of God without fault in a crooked and depraved generation, in which you shine like stars in the universe."

—Philippians 2:14-15 NIV

"May integrity and uprightness protect me, because my hope is in you."

—Psalm 25:21 NIV

"God will not prostitute His power to give us desires that will in the end be destructive to our walk with Him. But if we are consumed with a passion to find God's will through His Word and His Holy Spirit, we can always be in the place where God can shower down His power upon us."

David Jeremiah, *Sanctuary*

truth tips

Two Keys to Building Integrity

- **Get your eyes off the world.** Make an effort to feel secure in who God made you to be. Following the crowd just to fit in is one of Satan's traps. Vow to break the cycle NOW!

- **Allow the Holy Spirit and the truth of the Bible to saturate your heart, mind, and soul.** This is an essential key to building integrity.

leadership

" 'Whoever wants to become great
among you must be your servant, and
whoever wants to be first must be your
slave—just as the Son of Man did not
come to be served, but to serve.' "

—Matthew 20:26–28 NIV

"If anyone would come after me,
he must deny himself and take up his cross
daily and follow me. For whoever wants
to save his life will lose it, but whoever
loses his life for me will save it.' "

—Luke 9:23–24 NIV

wisdom past and present

"If the church is to prosper spiritually, she must
have spiritual leadership, not leadership by major-
ity vote. It is highly significant that when the apostle Paul found it necessary to ask for obedience
among the young churches, he never appealed to
them on the grounds that he had been duly elected
to office. He asserted his authority as an apostle

appointed by the Head of the church. He held his position by right of sheer spiritual ascendancy, the only earthly right that should be honored among the children of the new creation."

A.W. Tozer, *Tozer on Christian Leadership*

truth tips

How Christ Measures a Leader

▶ One who loves God with all one's heart, mind, and soul

▶ One who lays down one's life for others

▶ One who humbles oneself, taking on the very nature of a servant

▶ One who nurtures love, joy, peace, patience, kindness, goodness, faithfulness, gentleness, self-control

▶ One who walks with honor, integrity, holiness, purity

loving others

> "You shall not take vengeance, nor bear
> any grudge against the children of your
> people, but you shall love your neighbor
> as yourself: I am the LORD."
>
> —Leviticus 19:18 NKJV

> "No one has greater love than this, that
> someone would lay down his life for his
> friends. You are My friends if you do what
> I command you. I do not call you slaves
> anymore, because a slave doesn't know
> what his master is doing. I have called you
> friends, because I have made known to you
> everything I have heard from My Father."
>
> —John 15:13–15 HCSB

wisdom past and present

"After washing His disciples' feet, Jesus says, 'I have
given you an example so that you may copy what I
have done to you' (John 13:15). After giving
Himself as food and drink, he says, 'Do this in
remembrance of Me' (Luke 22:19 NIV). Jesus calls us
to continue His mission of revealing the perfect love

of God in this world. He calls us to total self-giving. He does not want us to keep anything for ourselves. Rather, He wants our love to be as full, as radical, and as complete as His own. He wants us to bend ourselves to the ground and touch the places in each other that most need washing. He also wants us to say to each other, 'Eat of me and drink of me.' By this complete mutual nurturing, He wants us to become one body and one spirit, united by the love of God."

Henri J. M. Nouwen, *Show Me the Way*

truth tips

A Can't-Miss Plan for Sharing Christian Love

▶ **Accept the call to care.** Think about modern-day outcasts: the glassy-eyed burnout at school or the geek who's always picked on in the halls. Would Jesus visit these people? Would He know their names, care about them, tell them stories? He would—and you should too.

▶ **Give a friend a love note.** Write "I love you" in six different languages: *"Je t' aime"* (French), *"Ti amo"* (Italian), *"Ai shite imasu"* (Japanese), *"Nagligivaget"* (Eskimo), *"Aloha wau ia oe"* (Hawaiian), *"S'agapo"* (Greek).

missions

" 'Go, therefore, and make disciples of all
nations, baptizing them in the name of the
Father and of the Son and the Holy Spirit,
teaching them to observe everything I have
commanded you. And remember, I am
with you always, to the end of the age.' "

—Matthew 28:19–20 HCSB

"As my Father hath sent me,
even so send I you."

—John 20:21 KJV

reality bytes

Andrew, 17, Charleston, South Carolina

"A summer mission trip to Venezuela
totally changed my life. I used to be afraid
to talk to people about my faith. Not
anymore. If I can do it here, I can do it any-
where! God also used this mission trip to
speak to me about my future. See, I've
been struggling with what to do with my
life. It's like there are a million options, but

how can you tell which one's the right one? Know what I mean? He helped me cut through all the fluff and really brought it down to the bottom line—you know— what's really important. See, it's not about 'How can I make the most money? Where can I work to be successful?' But it is about 'Where can I bleed and serve and sweat for You? Where can You send me to give? How can I be Your witness?' "

TRUTH TIPS

Thoughts About Mission Work

▶ **Take the time to look around you this week.** Someone needs you. Someone at church, at school, at home. There's that seventy-four-year-old whose wife has Alzheimer's disease. . . he needs someone to talk to. Then there's that couple with the handicapped child. . . they really could use a break.

▶ **You don't have to head off on a mission trip to Panama to be a missionary.** Be one to others in your life. Take the time to talk to that elderly man or to volunteer to baby-sit for that couple with a handicapped child.

parents

"He will turn the hearts of the fathers to their children, and the hearts of the children to their fathers; or else I will come and strike the land with a curse."

—Malachi 4:6 NIV

"Children, obey your parents in the Lord: for this is right. Honour thy father and mother; which is the first commandment with promise."

—Ephesians 6:1–2 KJV

truth tips

How to Make Peace with Your Parents

▶ **Don't shut down or put up a ten-foot thick wall between you and them.** This creates more tension. Instead, make an effort to talk to your parents about stuff that bugs you, as well as what's going on in your life.

▶ **Ask your parents to trust you with small decisions.** "After all, how else can I learn to recover from bad choices?" you can point out. "Let me learn plenty on the small stuff, so I can avoid the cost of messing up on the big stuff." But remember: Trust is like a two-way street. Gaining your parents' trust means being worthy of their trust.

▶ **Ask for "space."** Explain that every person—especially a teenager—needs escape from authority figures to reflect, think, make plans, communicate with God—alone.

persecuted people

> "There should be no division in the body. . . If one part suffers, every part suffers with it; if one part is honored, every part rejoices with it."
>
> —1 Corinthians 12:25–26 NIV

> "Remember those in prison as if you were their fellow prisoners, and those who are mistreated as if you yourselves were suffering."
>
> —Hebrews 13:3 NIV

reality bytes

Persecution in China

In the middle of the twentieth century, during the Communist revolution in China, a missionary and his son were captured by Communist soldiers, who threatened to kill the son unless the father denied his faith. He would not. The boy's hand was held, and with a slash of steel, four fingertips were taken. The boy screamed for his father. The military officer smiled and said,

"Now will you deny this Jesus?" "No," was the answer. Once again, the sword was raised and cut through flesh and bone, sinking deep into the wooden tabletop. The boy fainted in pain. "Oh, God!" the missionary cried. His heart wrenched, his eyes glazed with tears, and his face tightened. Staring at the floor, he whispered, "No, I will not deny Him." The officer commanded a soldier to shake the boy awake. He came to consciousness, screaming. Terror shone through his eyes as he searched for the father who held him when he cried, for the father who always comforted him. "Save me, Daddy! Save me!" the boy pleaded. The father's knees failed, and he slumped to the floor. "No—Jesus—please, no!" The soldier again raised his sword and took the boy's hand at the wrist.

When they later dug the graves and cast in the body parts, and then the bodies of the father and son, there had been no denial of Jesus the Lord.

This did not happen in the movies. It's not a fictional account. Sadly, it's reality. Religious persecution affects two hundred million people in more than sixty countries. Adapted from the book *Through Isaac's Eyes* by Daniel Barth Peters (Zondervan).

" 'But I say to you that whoever looks at a woman to lust for her has already committed adultery with her in his heart. If your right eye causes you to sin, pluck it out and cast it from you; for it is more profitable for you that one of your members perish, than for your whole body to be cast into hell. And if your right hand causes you to sin, cut it off and cast it from you; for it is more profitable for you that one of your members perish, than for your whole body to be cast into hell.' "

—Matthew 5:28–30 NKJV

"Flee from sexual immorality. . . . You are not your own; you were bought at a price. Therefore honor God with your body."

—1 Corinthians 6:18–20 NIV

why they matter

Stacie, 17, Boulder, Colorado

"I am committed to abstinence and purity. Someday I'm going to give my future husband everything. If you think about it, sex is like the only thing that you can completely save for your future mate. It is the one gift that I can give to him in perfect condition, and that thought makes it worth waiting for."

truth tips

How to Have Righteous Relationships

▶ **Stay on a purity path— and take a stand for abstinence.** It breaks God's heart when He sees how casually sex is treated, but it makes Him especially proud when He sees a young man or woman living right—remaining pure and respecting the opposite sex. Right now as a Christian teen, make a purity covenant with God. Even if you've already blown it sexually, ask God to help you remain pure from this point on.

▶ **Don't go out-of-bounds.** It's not a matter of how far you can go without sinning. Instead, your focus should be on purity—the standards God has set. Get this: Flirting with danger is a big mistake. Here are two key things that will help you:

▶ **Take up your sword and shield!** Use 1 Corinthians 6:18–20 as a "protective verse"—a spiritual shield. Repeat it in the face of temptation.

▶ **Take action.** Isn't it time to stop being defeated by Satan's lies? Let go of excuses—you know, lines like "It's a guy thing," or "It's okay because we're in love!"—and make a purity covenant with God.

school

i believe

"How beautiful upon the mountains are the feet of him who brings good news, who proclaims peace, who brings glad tidings of good things, who proclaims salvation, who says to Zion, 'Your God reigns!' "

—Isaiah 52:7 NKJV

"Dear friends, I urge you, as aliens and strangers in the world, to abstain from sinful desires, which war against your soul. Live such good lives among the pagans that, though they accuse you of doing wrong, they may see your good deeds and glorify God on the day he visits us."

—1 Peter 2:11–12 NIV

wisdom past and present

"Get out of your 'bunker' and get God back in school. Too many public schools are like war zones. The Enemy is on the prowl and is out to destroy as many students as possible. But you can fight back with the truth. Praying by your locker is a powerful weapon. It's also an amazing way to witness to your peers."

Tom Sipling, "30-Second Kneel Down," *Breakaway* magazine

truth tips

Know Your Rights

Did you know that the constitutions of both the United States and Canada protect your freedom of religious expression on a public school campus? Here are highlights of what you CAN do:

- Students can pray on a public school campus.
- Students can read their Bibles on a public school campus.
- Students can form religious clubs on campus if other noncurricular clubs exist.
- Students can hand out tracks, flyers, or other religious materials on campus.
- Students can do research papers, speeches, etc., with religious themes.
- Students can be exempt from participating in assignments that are contrary to their religious beliefs.
- Students can discuss religious issues although other students may overhear them.

servanthood

"Do not withhold good from those to whom it is due, when it is in your power to do it. Do not say to your neighbor, 'Go, and come back, and tomorrow I will give it.' "

—Proverbs 3:27–28 NASB

" 'So if I, the Master and Teacher, washed your feet, you must now wash each other's feet. I've laid down a pattern for you. What I've done, you do. I'm only pointing out the obvious. A servant is not ranked above his master; an employee doesn't give orders to the employer. If you understand what I'm telling you, act like it—and live a blessed life.' "

—John 13:14–17 THE MESSAGE

reality bytes

Putting Faith to WORK in West Virginia

Armed with hammers and paintbrushes, a battalion of 408 teens and youth workers have invaded Greenbrier County, West Virginia. Their mission: spend a week refurbishing more than sixty homes in this mountain community.

Just outside a rickety trailer house, Brian—a teen from Waukesha, Wisconsin—is playing ball with a five-year-old boy. "I want to help this child have a better place to live," the seventeen-year-old says. "This is why I'm here—for him."

In the process of sprucing up this boy's home, Brian and his crew from Group Workcamps build a much stronger foundation—the Gospel. (Group is a Christian ministry that gives teens a chance to get involved in service projects throughout the United States and Canada.)

"At each work site, we get a chance to build relationships with the people we serve," says seventeen-year-old Jeff of Hamilton, Michigan. "We tell them about our Savior. They not only hear our words, but they see our actions. And that's one of the best ways to spread the Gospel."

Sixteen-year-old Chris agrees. "The Bible says, 'whatever you did for one of the least of these brothers of mine, you did for me' " (Matthew 25:40 NIV), the Gurnee,

Illinois, teen pointed out. "I can't imagine sitting in front of the tube all summer. We've got to put our faith to work."

truth tips

Servanthood—Five Questions to Consider

▶ Would I dare to get out of my comfort zone for a couple of weeks during a mission trip. . . or for a church outreach?

▶ Would I dare to let God use me in a way that could change a life forever?

▶ Am I willing to say, "Break me, Lord. Use me in ways that stretch way beyond my imagination"?

▶ Do I care about those in need: the hurting, the hungry, the lonely?

▶ Am I willing to sacrifice my time—even my money—to impact a life for eternity?

transparency

" 'Not every one who says to me,
"Lord, Lord" will enter the kingdom of
heaven, but only he who does the will of
my Father who is in heaven. . . . Then
I will tell them plainly, "I never knew you.
Away from me, you evildoers!" ' "

—Matthew 7:21, 23 NIV

"For I am not ashamed of the gospel
of Christ, for it is the power of God to
salvation for everyone who believes, for
the Jew first and also for the Greek."

—Romans 1:16 NKJV

wisdom past and present

"The disciple living by grace rather than law has
undergone a decisive conversion—a turning
from mistrust to trust. The foremost characteris-
tic of living by grace is trust in the redeeming
work of Jesus Christ. To believe deeply, as Jesus
did, that God is present and at work in human
life is to understand that I am a beloved child of
this Father and hence, free to trust. That makes a

profound difference in the way I relate to myself and others; it makes an enormous difference in the way I live. To trust Abba, both in prayer and life, is to stand in childlike openness before a mystery of gracious love and acceptance."

Brennan Manning, *The Ragamuffin Gospel*

truth tips

How to Combat Phony Faith

▶ **Consider the word *Christian.*** It literally means, "Christ in one." If someone has truly received Christ in his or her heart, they'll be motivated to follow and obey Jesus.

▶ **Don't just "talk the walk" and not have Jesus in your heart.** The Bible makes it clear: Merely saying we are Christians can't give us eternal life. Only a committed, growing relationship with our Savior can do that.

▶ **Let Christ Search Your Heart.** Pray something like this: "Lord, help me to understood what distinguishes a 100% genuine Christian from a phony. Change my heart. Teach me to be real—with you and with others. Help me to live my faith in You. Amen."

witnessing

"For we are to God the fragrance of Christ among those who are being saved and among those who are perishing."

—2 Corinthians 2:15 NKJV

" 'You are the salt of the earth. . . . You are the light of the world. A city on a hill cannot be hidden. Neither do people light a lamp and put it under a bowl. Instead they put it on its stand, and it gives light to everyone in the house. In the same way, let your light shine before men, that they may see your good deeds and praise your Father in heaven.' "

—Matthew 5:13–16 NIV

wisdom past and present

"Jesus had the most open and all-encompassing mind that this world has ever seen. His own inner conviction was so strong, so firm, so unswerving that He could afford to mingle with any group secure in the knowledge that He would not be contaminated. It is fear that makes us unwilling to listen to another's point of view, fear that our own ideas may be attacked. Jesus had no such fear, no such pettiness of viewpoint, no need to fence Himself off for His own protection. He knew the difference between graciousness and compromise and we would do well to learn from Him. He set for us the most magnificent and glowing example of truth combined with mercy of all time, and in departing said: 'Go and do likewise' (Luke 10:37 NIV)."

Billy Graham, *Unto the Hills*

truth tips

Communicate with Confidence

▶ **Witnessing Key 1:** Relax! Sometimes Christians are way too uptight about witnessing. We fear we'll mess up what God accomplished through the cross. We obsess over appearances. We treat non-Christians like projects instead of people. We speak an alien language—known by insiders as "Christianese." The best thing you can do is relax and *live* what you believe, naturally, honestly, confidently.

▶ **Witnessing Key 2:** Be ready with answers—instead of just being polite and keeping quiet. Maybe your friends don't seem too interested in spiritual issues right now, but get this: They're watching you, especially your faith. And if they come to you with a question one day, you need to speak up.

▶ **Witnessing Key 3:** Have some backbone. Sometimes the best way of witnessing is with the word *NO*—"No thanks, I don't smoke, drink, chew [insert the appropriate word]"—then letting your backbone do the speaking for you.

words

"Do not let any unwholesome talk come out
of your mouths, but only what is helpful for
building others up according to their needs,
that it may benefit those who listen. . . .
Nor should there be obscenity, foolish talk
or coarse joking, which are out of place, but
rather thanksgiving."

—Ephesians 4:29, 5:4 NIV

"Consider how large a forest a small
fire ignites. And the tongue is a fire.
The tongue, a world of unrighteousness,
is placed among the parts of our bodies;
it pollutes the whole body, sets the course
of life on fire, and is set on fire by hell."

—James 3:5–6 HCSB

reality bytes

Keith, 14, Nashville, Tennessee

*"Why are other teens so cruel? Why do the
so-called cruel kids give me such a hard
time? Why can't we speak words of kindness to each other? Every day the questions*

race through my brain. You see, I'm a Christian in a school of unbelievers. I don't cuss or get into trouble. On top of that, I'm a musician—not an athlete. In fact, I hate gym. I'm the teen who is always picked last. Here's the crazy thing: At times, I've caught myself thinking that I'm weird because I'm creative and not athletic. What has saved me is the support I've gotten from my parents, my church, and my youth group.

"An amazing thing is starting to happen. As I learn to accept myself—and be confident in the person God made me to be—I'm slowly gaining acceptance from others. . .even from some of the guys who sometimes tease me. Above all, I'm striving to use words that build up others. I'm treating people the way I want to be treated."

truth tips

Some Words About Words

⫸ Regardless of what you say, whether it's good or bad, your words impact another person.

⫸ Jesus spoke so many things into being—just His words.

- Christians communicate their commitment to God through their actions as well as the words they choose.
- God wants believers to be committed to His Word.

workplace

"Do your best to present yourself to God
as one approved, a workman who does not
need to be ashamed and who correctly
handles the word of truth."

—2 Timothy 2:15 NIV

"But sanctify Christ as Lord in your
hearts, always being ready to make a
defense to everyone who asks you to give
an account for the hope that is in you,
yet with gentleness and reverence."

—1 Peter 3:15 NASB

wisdom past and present

"The Bible gives us countless examples of people
like Joseph, who not only served as an advisor to the
'president' of his day but also used that position to
influence the entire land. Can't we do that today?"

Bob Briner, *Roaring Lambs*

truth tips

How to Witness at Work

Your workplace is a mission field. But you don't have to hand out tracts to tell others about your faith in Jesus Christ. Instead, drop a few signals:

- Ask questions: "Does your family have any Christmas (or Easter) traditions? We go to church on Christmas Eve and. . ."

- When someone mentions a struggle they're going through, let them know you'll pray for them. How? A short note or quick word is often all it takes.

- Let your actions speak loudly. Your tasks at work come first. If you're not a good employee, you may end up giving all Christians a bad name.

- When other workers start telling off-color jokes or making crude remarks, fight the urge to participate. Don't act superior or judgmental (after all, non-Christians *will* act like non-Christians). In other words, model integrity—and model Christ.

bibliography

books

Abegg, Jimmy. *Ragamuffin Prayers*. Harvest House, 2000.

Asimakoupoulos, Greg. *Heroic Faith*. W Publishing Group, 2002.

Assisi, St. Francis of. *Ragamuffin Prayers*. Harvest House, 2000.

Blackaby, Henry T. *Experiencing God Day-by-Day*. Broadman & Holman, 1998.

Bonhoeffer, Dietrich. *The Cost of Discipleship*. Collier Books, 1959.

Briner, Bob. *Roaring Lambs*. Zondervan, 1993.

Bryan, William Jennings. *Life by Design*. J. Countryman, 2002.

Card, Michael. *Immanuel: Reflections on the Life of Christ*. Thomas Nelson, 1981.

Chambers, Oswald. *My Utmost for His Highest*. Dodd, Mead & Company, 1935.

Davidman, Joy. *Smoke on the Mountain*. Westminster Press, 1954.

Davis, Ken. *How to Live with Your Parents without Losing Your Mind*. Zondervan, 1988.

Dobson, James. *Preparing for Adolescence*. Regal Books, 1989.

Dolan, Dave. *Get Real, Get Ready, Get Going*. Fleming H. Revell, 1999.

Duncan, Todd. *Life by Design*. J. Countryman, 2002.

Eldredge, John. *Dare to Desire*. J. Countryman, 2002.

Exley, Richard. *Your Bridge to a Better Future*. Thomas Nelson, 1997.

Graham, Billy. *Unto the Hills*. Word Publishing, 1986.

i believe

Graham, Franklin. *Living Beyond the Limits*. Thomas Nelson, 1998.

Haggard, Ted. *Loving Your City Into the Kingdom*. Regal Books, 1997.

Jeremiah, David. *Sanctuary*. Integrity, 2002.

Keaggy, Phil. *Faith That Breathes*. Barbour, 2003.

Keller, Helen. *Your Bridge to a Better Future*. Thomas Nelson, 1997.

Le Mee, Katharine. *Chant*. Bell Tower, 1994.

Lewis, C. S. *A Grief Observed*. Bantam, 1976.

———. *An Experiment in Criticism*. Cambridge University Press, 1961.

———. *Letters of C. S. Lewis*. Harcourt Brace Jovanovich, 1966.

———. *Letters to Malcolm: Chiefly on Prayer*. Harcourt Brace Jovanovich, 1964.

———. *Mere Christianity*. HarperCollins, 2001.

———. *Miracles*. Macmillan, 1960.

Lucado, Max. *Grace for the Moment*. J. Countryman, 2000.

———. *He Still Moves Stones*. Word Publishing, 1993.

Manning, Brennan. *The Ragamuffin Gospel*. Multnomah, 1990.

May, Gerald G. *Addiction and Grace*. Harper, 1988.

McGee, Robert S. *The Search for Significance*. Word Publishing, 1998.

Miller, Calvin. *Once Upon a Tree*. Howard, 2002.

Moreau, A. Scott. *Essentials of Spiritual Warfare*. Harold Shaw, 1997.

Mother Teresa. *Mother Teresa: Contemplative in the Heart of the World*. Servant, 1985.

———. *Your Bridge to a Better Future*. Thomas Nelson, 1997.

Mullins, Rich. *Rich Mullins: An Arrow Pointing to Heaven*, Broadman & Holman, 2000.

Nouwen, Henri J. M. *Show Me the Way*. The Crossroad Publishing Company, 1995.

Packer, J. I. *J. I. Packer Answers Questions for Today*. Tyndale House, 2001.

————. *Knowing God*. InterVarsity Press, 1973.

Patterson, Eugene. *Earth & Altar*. InterVarsity Press, 1985.

Peters, Daniel Barth. *Through Isaac's Eyes*. Zondervan, 1996.

Redman, Matt. *The Unquenchable Worshipper*. Regal Books, 2001.

Smith, Aaron. *Ragamuffin Prayers*. Harvest House, 2000.

Smith, Michael W. *Ragamuffin Prayers*. Harvest House, 2000.

Spurgeon, Charles H. *All of Grace*. Moody, 1992.

————. *Morning and Evening*. Thomas Nelson, 1994.

Singh, Sundar. *Jesus Freaks*. Bethany House, 2002.

Tada, Joni Eareckson. *When God Weeps*. Zondervan, 1997.

Tozer, A. W. *Tozer on Christian Leadership*. Christian Publications, 2001.

Wilkerson, David. *Victory Over Sin and Self*. Fleming H. Revell, 1980.

Wilkinson, Bruce H., *Youthwalk Again*. Zondervan, 1993.

Yount, David. *Breaking Through God's Silence*. Touchstone, 1997.

articles

Bush, George W. Speech at Tsinghua University in China, Feb. 22, 2002.

Cleary, T. J. "Taming Your Temper." *Breakaway*, November 1999.

"Crossculture Christians." *Breakaway*, November 1997.

"Defeating a Killer." *Breakaway*, February 2001.

Holmgren, Mike. "Breakaway's Guide to an Amazing Life." *Breakaway*, May 2003.

Huston, Todd. "More Than Mountains." *Breakaway*, August 1996.

Koehler, Manfred. "When Change Scares You." *Breakaway*, January 2002.

Sipling, Tom. "30-Second Kneel Down." *Breakaway*, September 2001.

Von Braun, Wernher. "Tried and Transfigured." *Reader's Digest*, June 1960.

about the authors

Terry Brown is a former nurse and the creator of children's and youth product, including *Communicate* and the Today's Girls book series. She lives in Muncie, Indiana, with her husband and three teenage sons.

Michael Ross is the editor of Focus on the Family's *Breakaway* magazine. He is also the author of several books for young people and families, including *Geek-Proof Your Faith* and *Faith Encounter*. Michael lives in Colorado Springs with his wife and son.

if you enjoyed
I Believe,
check out
Communicate.

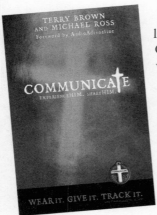

Christianity is more than a lifestyle. It's a relationship with the Creator of the universe—and that's worth passing along. Especially for teens, *Communicate—Experience Him. Share Him* focuses on the two-part reality of godly living— knowing Christ in a personal, intimate way, and telling others about Him by word and deed. *Communicate* will help to equip the "new generation" to live out the Great Commission.